F·R·I·E·N·D·S

THE TELEVISION SERIES

THE OFFICIAL COOKBOOK

F·R·I·E·N·D·S
THE TELEVISION SERIES

CENTRAL PERK

THE OFFICIAL COOKBOOK

WRITTEN BY KARA MICKELSON

TITAN
BOOKS

AN INSIGHT EDITIONS BOOK

Contents

Introduction

Although there are many iconic and well-known places throughout the ten seasons of *Friends*, there's something uniquely comforting and special about Central Perk, the coffee shop where the characters frequently meet up. It's a home away from home, a warm, inviting place where the gang comes together to enjoy a delicious cup of joe and spend time with each other. It's a place where Rachel gets her first job, where she has her first romantic kiss with Ross, and where the friends tease Chandler about his vocal inflections. These moments are often shared over a cup of coffee, a latte, or a blueberry muffin.

Reflecting on today's coffee culture, it's curious how much of it may have been inspired by Central Perk. Many of us shared in the wacky, fun, sad, and joyful moments of the friends' lives, often relatable to our own on so many levels. Coffee and culture are inherently intertwined today, whether in neighborhood coffeehouses to cities around the globe, or at our own kitchen table.

The deep social connections we cultivate over coffee, small bites, and treats might be why the coffee craze has persisted and evolved over the years. From the early sixteenth-century Turkish coffeehouses to European salons for intellectual pursuits and creative endeavors, places dedicated to gathering and socializing while sipping a delicious brew are not new.

From enjoying humble beginnings like a latte, café au lait, or cappuccino, we've moved on to matcha, decadent sweet-cream foam, alternative plant and nut milks, fancy pour overs, cold brews, boba or bubble tea, lavender peppermint, and even ube lattes. Today we aren't just high on the caffeine and sugar or easy grab-and-go fare; we still long for the familiar connection that coffeehouses and places like Central Perk inspire. We still love that "thing" that was captured on the show. And what exactly was that "thing"? Perhaps it's as simple as sharing, connection, and the proverbial "coffee break" from whatever ails us.

A delicious cup of coffee doesn't just help us get through the day. It's a way to slow down, take stock of our time, and savor the moment. From that first ethereal sip in the morning to a midday pick-me-up or a late-night boost, it's a nod to something subtle yet significant. That "go, go, go" state of being is the pretext, but the real fix is in letting go and taking a time-out.

With modern communication tools, most of us are wired 24/7. My hope is this cookbook creates opportunities to spend time with friends, to share and expand the deeper, more personal connections we crave outside the technology we're so dependent upon. Those connections are at the beating heart of coffeehouses as well as coffee at home. It's what keeps the trend alive.

These pages are filled with personalized drinks, both warm and cool, some with exotic ingredients, and pastries, snacks, and treats all made with care and intention, calling you to make space in your day for something comforting and maybe even something new, all while celebrating beloved moments from *Friends*.

Explore the recipes in this book with the same twentysomething zeal and excitement that Rachel, Monica, Phoebe, Ross, Chandler, and Joey had for life—the zeal that drew us to the show. On the other side of each cooking adventure, our real friends are cheering us on and supporting our endeavors big and small. The stories we create together iron out the rough edges of life and make each day memorable. Whether it's a "nailed it" moment, a happy accident, or a resounding success, make embarking on each recipe in this book a fun way to reward yourself, share, reminisce, craft new stories, and make memories to savor.

When we open our home and kitchen, whether we are making a beverage for one or planning a game night, girls' night, or hangout with friends, these recipes can be used as they are written or, if you're a chef like Monica, as a foundation for a new personalized creation. Be fearless—like Rachel—and dive in and have fun.

{ MAGIC BEANS }

What does it take to make the perfect brew?

It's a complicated question with excessive amounts of information to wade through before getting a satisfactory answer. Without risking a funny Ross moment, like when he painfully tries to explain unagi, incorrectly I might add, it's best to stick to the basics when it comes to the recipes in this cookbook. Delving into coffee culture can easily send you down a rabbit hole of information, so we've gathered some basic terms here and a drink ratio guide to get you started.

COFFEE BASICS

When it comes to coffee, mastering a few key components will set you up for success. Espresso is key, as most specialty coffee drinks use espresso as the base. A pour-over coffee will work well for the blended and cold coffee recipes in this cookbook. If you don't have a pod/capsule machine or a fancy espresso maker, a small investment in a stovetop espresso maker will help get you to the finish line, without breaking the bank. There are also powdered espresso options available that you can use in a pinch.

ESPRESSO

Espresso is a very concentrated type of coffee with an efficient extraction method that exposes more of the surface area of the ground beans to the water. A typical shot of espresso is 1 to 1½ ounces, versus a standard 8-ounce cup of filter coffee. It takes about 25 to 30 seconds to pull a shot of espresso. The brewing method for espresso uses a machine to send pressurized near-boiling water (195°F to 205°F) through tightly packed and finely ground beans. Here, it's all about technique, traditionally beginning with roasting the beans longer than drip coffee beans. Espresso can, however, be made from any type of coffee beans, as long as they are ground to the appropriately fine texture. The hit of caffeine in espresso is relative to its size and quick consumption. A typical single espresso shot has less caffeine than a full 8-ounce cup of filter coffee. Although it's called a shot, it's still a sipping beverage meant to be savored. A proper, well-prepared shot will have a crema, or caramel-colored, creamy foam layer, on top.

COLD BREW

Cold brew is chilled coffee made from very coarse grounds (almost the same consistency as coarse sand or bread crumbs) that have been steeped in room-temperature or cold water for 12 to 24 hours.

POUR OVER

Done by hand, this is a refined and precise technique in which water is poured over ground coffee. The technique offers more control than a standard coffee maker. Connoisseurs prefer the complete control this method gives them in perfecting their ideal brew. It's a longer brewing process, but it results in more complex flavor notes than can be achieved on a standard home machine. Cold brew can also be made using a modified pour-over technique.

GUIDE TO BASIC DRINK RATIOS

Study this guide to basic drink ratios like Joey studies his lines. Not all the coffees listed below are included in the recipes in this book, but as the producer in your own coffeehouse scene, you can ad-lib and make your own creations.

ESPRESSO (SOLO)
One shot of espresso served in an espresso, or demitasse, cup.

DOUBLE ESPRESSO (DOPPIO)
Double shot of espresso served in an espresso cup.

SHORT OR CAFÉ MACCHIATO
One shot of espresso, a dollop of steamed milk (1 to 2 ounces), and foam. Basically, this is a solo or doppio espresso shot with a very small amount of steamed milk and a dollop of foam on top.

LATTE OR LONG MACCHIATO
Two shots of espresso, a dollop of steamed milk, and foam. The shot is poured over the steamed milk, creating the signature mark in the center.

RISTRETTO
One shot of espresso with half the water, making it more concentrated.

RED EYE
One shot of espresso added to filtered coffee. A popular term before double shots became the standard espresso pull.

LONG BLACK
Espresso pulled directly into the water to preserve the crema. It contains about 3 to 4 ounces of water to one or two shots of espresso.

AMERICANO
Similar to a long black, but the espresso is added before the water. It typically contains 6 to 12 ounces of water.

CAFÉ OR CLASSIC LATTE
One or two shots of espresso, steamed milk, with foam on top, but less foam and more steamed milk than a cappuccino or latte macchiato.

CAPPUCCINO
One shot of espresso, steamed milk, and double the foam of a latte. It is typically one-third single or double espresso. The ratio is one-third steamed milk, one-third frothed milk, one-third espresso.

FLAT WHITE
One or two shots of espresso, steamed milk, but no foam.

MOCHA
One shot of espresso, chocolate powder, steamed milk, and extra foam.

AFFOGATO
One scoop vanilla ice cream, one or two shots of espresso over the top, and optional Italian liqueur (such as amaretto or Frangelico).

Espresso

Latte

Cappuccino

Americano

BASIC TERMS

This glossary will keep you in the know and make you a better server, like Rachel. You might even get a promotion to head barista or run the coffeehouse, like Gunther.

BREW TEMPERATURE
The general consensus is that espresso should be brewed with water with a temperature between 190°F and 205°F in order to obtain optimal extraction.

BREW TIME
Brew time is one indicator of a good espresso shot. It's calculated from the moment the brewing begins until the action stops. Traditionally espresso takes between 25 and 30 seconds to make.

PULL
A pull is the actual brewing of a shot of espresso. Think of pulling on a lever of a traditional espresso machine. Today a simple push of a button will start the process, although the term *pull* is still used to describe the action of making an espresso.

CREMA
Crema is a caramel-colored creamy top layer of foam that is a sign of a good espresso. Crema is created by the dispersion of gases in liquid at a high pressure. The liquid contains emulsified oils that form the crema layer.

DOSAGE
This refers to the amount of ground coffee used to produce a shot of espresso, typically 7 grams per 1 to 1½ ounces for a single espresso shot.

FOAM/FROTH
MICROFOAM is hundreds of thousands of ultrafine steamed milk bubbles, poured over a single or double espresso. It adds a silky, velvety texture. Milk heated to between 139°F and 149°F adds a pleasing complement to a strong brew, cutting through the bitterness. It's used for latte art, lattes, and cappuccinos.

FROTHED MILKED is whipped to create a layer of microfine bubbles, creating an airy texture, and can be hot or cold. Frothed milk is airy, like shaving cream. The airy, dryer, texture of frothed milk is used to make lattes, cappuccinos, and macchiatos by floating the milk foam on top of the steamed milk and espresso.

STEAMED MILK is heavier, velvety, creamy, hot microfoam (like melted ice cream).

GRIND
The size of the coffee grounds is relevant to the desired end product. Espresso uses a fine grind, whereas cold brew uses a very coarse grind.

Basic EQUIPMENT NEEDS

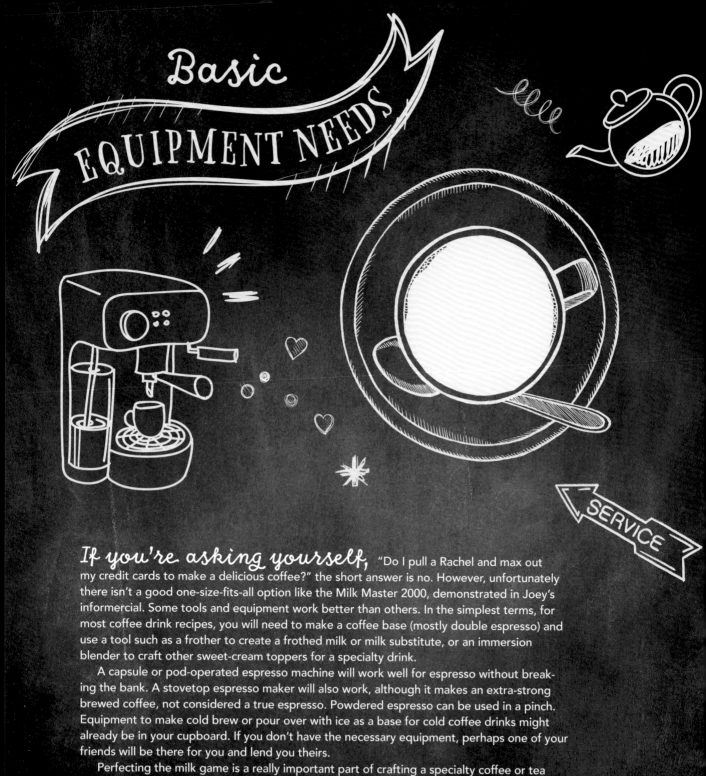

If you're asking yourself, "Do I pull a Rachel and max out my credit cards to make a delicious coffee?" the short answer is no. However, unfortunately there isn't a good one-size-fits-all option like the Milk Master 2000, demonstrated in Joey's informercial. Some tools and equipment work better than others. In the simplest terms, for most coffee drink recipes, you will need to make a coffee base (mostly double espresso) and use a tool such as a frother to create a frothed milk or milk substitute, or an immersion blender to craft other sweet-cream toppers for a specialty drink.

A capsule or pod-operated espresso machine will work well for espresso without breaking the bank. A stovetop espresso maker will also work, although it makes an extra-strong brewed coffee, not considered a true espresso. Powdered espresso can be used in a pinch. Equipment to make cold brew or pour over with ice as a base for cold coffee drinks might already be in your cupboard. If you don't have the necessary equipment, perhaps one of your friends will be there for you and lend you theirs.

Perfecting the milk game is a really important part of crafting a specialty coffee or tea drink. While there are many options to help you achieve a nice layer of froth, some tools work better than others for getting that silky, velvety foam texture. Feel free to mix and match milk techniques required in a specific recipe. Use one of the basic ratios (see page 11) of a specialty coffee as a guide. It's easy to make a latte into a cappuccino or a macchiato. Many hot drinks can be made cold and vice versa. With practice you will find out what works best and what style of milk and topper best suits your coffee style and taste.

ESPRESSO MACHINES

PROFESSIONAL HOME-STYLE ESPRESSO MACHINES

These machines are a luxury and are available at varying price points. The benefits of these machines, beside looking uber-hip in the kitchen, allow you to customize the end product.

AUTOMATIC ESPRESSO MACHINES (SEMI- AND SUPERAUTOMATIC)

Depending on the style and price point, some of these machines have automated functions while others are programmed into the machine by the user. Functions, such as the espresso pull and milk frothing, and key features, such as drink size and grind size, can be relegated to the push of a button.

CAPSULE MACHINES

A capsule espresso maker uses capsules or pods filled with premeasured coffee to make espresso or other espresso drinks. They remove the guesswork, other than where and when to buy the refills.

STOVETOP ESPRESSO MAKER

These coffee makers will brew three to twelve small cups of strong espresso-like coffee on the stovetop. They are small, easy to use, and affordable. Using one is as simple as filling it with water, adding in fine- to medium-grind coffee beans, and placing on the stove.

FILTER COFFEE DEVICES

POUR OVER

The traditional Chemex brand pour-over device makes a regular showing in many *Friends* episodes, although there are plenty of models to choose from. The concept is similar to a drip-coffee machine, with the added ability to regulate the water temperature, pouring speed, brew ratio of coffee to water, and coffee-grind size. The method requires a special funnel, filters, temperature sensor, scale, and a kettle with a thin gooseneck spout. Once you have perfected the temperature, pouring technique, and brew process, you are ready to go! But don't shy away from this method, as many coffee connoisseurs praise it for achieving the perfect brew.

COLD BREW

Ideally, a cold brew is sweet and bold, less bitter, and less acidic than an equivalent hot brewed coffee. The flavor is concentrated and holds up well in iced drinks and is less watered down than iced coffee made the traditional way. Cold brew can be used to make coffee soda or warm coffee (by adding some hot water), or as a base for other drinks. To make cold brew, a large French press or glass canister with a lid is preferred. If using a large glass canister, use a cotton cone filter or nut-milk bag to contain and secure the coarse coffee grounds.

OTHER EQUIPMENT

GRINDER

Grinding your own coffee beans guarantees a fresher, better-tasting, and more flavorful cup of joe. Look for a grinder that has multiple grind settings to achieve the perfect consistent grind size, whether fine for espresso, medium for pour over, or extra coarse for cold brew. Some grinders have digital timers, built-in scales, and dosing options.

ELECTRIC FROTHER

An electric frother works well for compact, small carafes. Add milk and press a button, and the electric frother whisks, foams, and heats the milk. Some offer options to steam or froth milk. This method is quick and convenient for traditional lattes and cappuccinos as well as for heating matcha. Please note, though, that they do not have enough power to create sweet cream, coconut cream, or cheese foam.

BATTERY-OPERATED HANDHELD WAND/ WHISK

Battery-operated and handheld wand frothers and whisks are inexpensive options that work well for traditional frothed drinks once the milk is heated. Depending on the brand, the whisk will create airy microfoam from milk and milk alternatives, although the battery-operated wand will not have enough strength to whip up sweet cream, coconut cream, or cheese foam.

PUMP-STYLE FROTHER

Glass or stainless steel pitchers with a lid-type plunger will froth hot or cold milk. They work best with nonfat milk rather than whole. If using a glass pitcher, the milk is added to the pitcher and heated in the microwave. For the stainless steel version, the milk is heated separately. It takes about 40 seconds to create a velvety microfoam with the pump. Without a whisk, this frother adds air to the milk through pumping with the plunge filter by hand and heating the milk in the microwave or stovetop.

IMMERSION BLENDER

Use a tall container (typically sold with the blender) and a whisk attachment to make whipped coffee Dalgona style, or sweet cream, cheese foam, and whipped cream. The single whisk attachment and small container are perfect for single-serve drinks and heavier dairy or coconut cream–based toppings.

HANDHELD MIXER

This is the next best option to an immersion blender for making specialty coffees. Also, it's an important tool for making desserts that require small-batch mixing.

STAND MIXER

Many of the recipes in this cookbook call for a stand mixer. A whisk attachment, paddle attachment, and dough hook will make the preparation easier, although it's possible to use a handheld mixer and good old-fashioned muscle, for most recipes, to get the job done.

PITCHERS

A 2-cup glass measuring pitcher, for heating liquid in a microwave, is useful for many of the recipes. A 12-ounce stainless steel pitcher is great for steaming milk, if you have a steam wand with your coffee maker, and for making sugar paste.

CANDY, QUICK READ, OR DEEP-FRY THERMOMETER

Use these to check the oil temperature for frying, and other temperatures, during the cooking or baking process.

KITCHEN SCALE

Use a kitchen scale to measure beans, flours, butter, and sugar. Weight measurements tend to be more accurate than volume measurements, especially when it comes to baking.

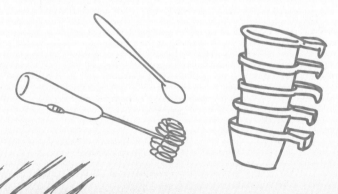

KITCHEN CONVERSIONS

1 TBSP:
3 TSP

1 GALLON:
4 QUARTS
8 PINTS
16 CUPS
128 OUNCES
3.8 LITERS

1 QUART:
2 PINTS
4 CUPS
32 OUNCES
0.95 LITERS

1 PINT:
2 CUPS
16 OUNCES
480 ML

CUP	OZ	TBSP	TSP
1	8	16	48
3/4	6	12	36
2/3	5	11	32
1/2	4	8	24
1/3	3	5	16
1/4	2	4	12

1 CUP:
8 OUNCES
240 ML
16 TBSP

¼ CUP:
4 TBSP
2 OUNCES
60 ML

Baking Note: Volume measurements and weight measurements are not always interchangeable or equal due to density of ingredients.

FRIENDS SHARE

Chef Monica's Culinary Tips & Terms

Let Chef Monica guide you in the kitchen by offering some of her favorite tips and reviewing some important culinary terms.

BLIND BAKING

To cook or partially cook pastry dough without a filling. This technique prevents soggy crusts by parcooking (partially cooking) pastry dough and tart shells before filling with a cooked filling, such as a custard.

CAKE FLOUR

Cake flour is significantly finer than all-purpose and bread flours, absorbs more water, and has lower protein and gluten content, which add lift to baked goods and leads to a more delicate crumb. It also adds a desirable light, airy texture. To substitute cake flour for all-purpose flour in recipes, add an additional 2 tablespoons of cake flour to what the recipe calls for.

00 FLOUR

This flour has a very fine, powdery texture. A high-protein flour, it creates a chewy, crisp crust great for flatbreads and pizzas that require high temperature when cooking.

ALL-PURPOSE FLOUR

All-purpose flour is a combination of hard and soft wheats. The texture is denser than cake flour, adding structure and stability to baked goods. When working with all-purpose flour, it will feel heavier and stickier than cake flour.

BREAD FLOUR

This high-protein and high-gluten flour increases gluten's elasticity, and the extra structure and chewy texture is perfect for yeasted breads and leavened doughs like pretzels and even croissants.

BUCKWHEAT FLOUR

Buckwheat is not a wheat but rather a fruit related to rhubarb, contrary to its name. It is naturally gluten-free and is delicious in baked goods, adding extra depth of flavor to cookies, pastries, and breads, or it can be a main component in crêpes, pancakes, and soba noodles. It has a slightly nutty flavor when baked.

YEAST

Yeast adds lift to baked goods by consuming sugar and producing carbon dioxide and alcohol. This fermentation process causes dough to expand. Proofing yeast essentially means to test and activate the yeast. Not all yeast needs to be proofed, but it's preferable to hydrate it. Rapid-rise and quick-rise yeast aren't typically proofed, as it takes away from the yeast activation when dissolving in liquid. If you haven't baked with yeast before, it's worth sacrificing a bit of lift by hydrating instant brands and active dry yeast to confirm that the yeast is active before proceeding with a recipe.

Ideally, use the type of yeast stated in the recipe, but generally it is possible to convert to another type if needed. To convert, use 1 teaspoon instant yeast to 1¼ teaspoons active dry, or 1 teaspoon active dry to ¾ teaspoon instant yeast. Once opened, yeast is best stored in the freezer. Store a small amount in the refrigerator for convenience as cold yeast takes longer to activate.

PROOFING BOX

Yeasted or leavened doughs are typically proofed after the final shaping. It's the final stage in the proofing process. Use a plastic container with a lid that will accommodate the shaped dough on a sheet tray and include a heatproof container to hold boiling water. Alternatively, the oven works as well. Just turn the light on (leave the oven off). The benefit of having a separate proofing box is that the oven is free during a longer proof.

MERINGUE

Meringue is stiffly whipped egg whites. Use egg whites separated from eggs, rather than a carton of egg whites, which may have additives. Separate eggs by cracking the egg into your clean hand and letting the whites carefully drip through your fingers into a clean bowl. Always crack and separate an egg into a clean bowl, as any yolk will ruin the meringue. Reserve egg yolks for other baked goods (some recipes call for an egg wash, which requires an egg yolk). Freeze egg whites overnight and use them defrosted at room temperature for more stable peaks.

Make sure all the equipment and tools you're using for making meringue are clean and free from any grease. Wipe tools and equipment down with white vinegar and dry thoroughly before whisking or using with egg whites. It's best to use a stand mixer or handheld mixer to make meringue, due to the extended whisking time required. Note that the line between medium peaks, stiff peaks, and overwhipped egg whites is small, so don't leave the mixer running and walk away. There isn't a fix for broken meringue.

GINGER

To peel ginger, use the side edge of a teaspoon to peel and scrape off the paperlike skin from the knobby rhizome. This approach leaves you with more ginger than using a knife.

GANACHE

Ganache is often used for toppings, candy truffles, and frosting, and as a base for many desserts. Classic ganache is made with heavy cream; however, it may also be made with many milk alternatives or sweetened condensed milk, depending on the desired thickness, taste, and end use. The standard chocolate to heavy cream ratio for ganache is 1:1, although adjustments can be made to achieve a desired thickness and texture. Follow the recipe as written for best results.

TEMPER

Tempering means "to stabilize." Properly tempered chocolate will snap and have a shiny, glossy, and smooth appearance and harden from a melted state within 3 to 5 minutes. Once tempered, chocolate will hold its shape and not melt as quickly when handled. Liquids can also be tempered, minimizing the risk of overheating that would break or curdle a sauce or custard. Ingredients with very different temperatures are tempered by introducing a small portion of one ingredient to the other before combining all the ingredients together. It is essentially slowly introducing hot and cool ingredients to each other in a systematic way for the best end result.

MISE EN PLACE

This French term translates to "everything in its place." Establishing your mise en place is the foundation of a well-operating kitchen, something Monica surely knows. Read recipes through at least once. Gather the equipment, tools, and supplies you'll need. Prepare all the ingredients, label them, and place them in order of use on a tray before getting started.

PINCH

A pinch is between 1/16 and 1/8 teaspoon. It's the amount you can hold between two fingers.

ROOM TEMPERATURE

Room temperature is between 71°F and 81°F. This is the best temperature for baking ingredients when room temperature is called for, and for proofing dough. Most baking ingredients should be at room temperature before baking; however, it's important to still maintain ingredients in a food-safe temperature.

FRY STATION

Use a large heavy pot for oil that allows room for food to float and not crowd. Don't fill the pot more than two-thirds full with oil. Heat oil slowly. Monitor the temperature of oil with a deep-fry or a candy thermometer. The ideal fry temperature is generally between 350°F to 375°F to create a crisp exterior and moist interior for the food. There are some exceptions, like par-frying French fries at 325°F, with the second fry at 400°F. Fry a single portion of food and adjust the temperature up or down as needed. Make sure the interior of the food is cooked throughout unless it will be cooked in the oven after frying. To set up a fry station, clear your work area. Line a sheet tray(s) with paper towels for fried items to drain on. Have a skimmer, slotted spoon, and/or long tongs available. Keep tools clean and dry as water will cause oil to splatter. Use an oil with a high smoke point, such as peanut, canola, sunflower, safflower, corn, or some vegetable oil (not olive oil). Use enough oil to submerge food. Cooled oil can be strained and reused, depending on what was cooked in it. Maintain the proper oil temperature. Cold food will lower the fry temperature quickly. Let the oil heat back up between batches. And most importantly, don't leave oil unattended!

HONEY POWDER/GRANULES

This blend of dried honey and sugar can be used to sweeten candied nuts, sweet cream, whipped coffee, specialty coffees, and teas. Purchase online or at Asian markets.

MAPLE POWDER/SUGAR

This pure maple sugar in a granule form can be used as a sweetener for candied nuts, sweet cream, whipped coffee, specialty coffee, and teas. Purchase online or at specialty markets.

Basic Recipes

COLD BREW

YIELD: About 4 cups (32 ounces)
PREP & COOK TIME: 12 to 18 hours or overnight

USED IN: Ross's Dark & Stormy Coconut Blended Cold Brew (page 65), Rachel's Vanilla Sweet Cream Cold Brew (page 67)

1 cup very coarse ground coffee (with a bread crumb texture)
4 cups (32 ounces) cold or room temperature filtered water

NOTE: Filter bags can be purchased online. Nut-milk filter bags are preferred.

Fit a cloth cold brew filter or nut bag in a large 5 to 6 cup glass canister. Drape the edge of the filter bag over the rim of the canister, leaving an opening for the grounds. Tie a piece of string around the filter, if needed, to secure the bag to the edge of canister. Fill the filter bag with the coffee. Slowly add the water. Transfer to the refrigerator and steep overnight or between 12 to 18 hours, depending on the desired strength. Remove the filter, cover the cold brew with a lid, and refrigerate.

The standard ratio of coffee to water is 1:4, but it can be adjusted as desired. Keep in mind, with this method the water drips through the filter, immersing the filter bag and coffee grounds in water, so the size of the container in relation to the amount of water is important.

If using a French press, add the coffee to the French press, then add the water. Let steep in the refrigerator. After steeping, press down the filter and pour the cold brew into a fresh glass container with a lid.

Store in the refrigerator for up to 2 weeks. The flavor will degrade after the first week. To prolong freshness, downsize the storage container as you consume the coffee to reduce the airflow in the container.

SALTED CARAMEL SAUCE

YIELD: About 1½ cups
PREP & COOK TIME: 20 minutes, plus time to cool

USED IN: Rachel's Vanilla Sweet Cream Cold Brew (page 67), Monica's Perfect Poached Spiced Candied Apple (page 169)

1 cup granulated sugar
1 teaspoon salt
¼ cup water or apple cider
4 tablespoons unsalted butter, cubed
⅓ cup heavy cream
1 teaspoon powdered espresso (optional)

In a medium stainless or light-colored saucepan over medium heat, combine the sugar, salt, and water and bring the mixture to a boil while stirring frequently, about 6 minutes. Increase the heat to medium-high and cook to a golden caramel brown without stirring, 7 to 10 minutes. Remove from the heat and stir in the butter and cream. The mixture will rise and bubble. Let the mixture cool and stir in the espresso powder now, if using. Transfer it to a covered container. The sauce will thicken as it cools. The sauce can be stored in a tightly covered container for 3 to 4 weeks in the refrigerator. Warm slightly to thin before using.

BASIC SIMPLE SYRUP

YIELD: About ½ cup
PREP & COOK TIME: 10 minutes

1 cup granulated sugar
1 cup water
½ cup raw, unsalted nuts
   (optional)

In a small saucepan over medium heat, combine the sugar and water and bring to a simmer. Stir until the sugar is dissolved, 3 to 5 minutes. Remove from the heat and let cool completely. If not using right away, the syrup can be stored in a covered container in the refrigerator for up to 1 month. Add a ½ teaspoon of water to thin the syrup, if needed, before using.

For a nut-infused syrup, add the nuts to the sugar and water and strain once the syrup is cooked. Nut syrup will crystalize and needs to be used the day it is made. Strained nuts can be used for Eddie's Angry Dried Fruit & Sweetened Nuts (page 100).

NOTES: This recipe uses a 1:1 ratio of sugar to water. If using honey instead of sugar, reduce the water by ⅓ cup. Instead of a nut-based syrup, try flavoring the drinks with infused milks like Hazelnut Oat Milk (page 31) used in Rachel's Blackout Latte (page 61).

BASIC PIADINA FLATBREAD

YIELD: Two 7-inch flatbreads
PREP & COOK TIME: 1 hour

USED IN: Rachel's Fire Grilled Veggie Flatbread (page 116), Joey's "Don't Be Jelly!" Fish Piadina Sandwich (page 125), Rachel's Grilled Shrimp Cobb Salad Wraps for Two—Extra Tip (page 129)

⅛ teaspoon granulated sugar

1¼ cups 00 flour or all-purpose flour, plus more as needed for dough and dusting

¼ cup cold, defrosted duck fat or buttered-flavored shortening, lard, or olive oil, plus more for the pan

¼ to ½ cup warm water

¼ teaspoon salt

In a large bowl, whisk the sugar and flour together. Make a well in the center of the flour. Add the duck fat and ¼ cup warm water to the well. Sprinkle the salt on the outer edge of the well.

Using your hands, massage the fat with the water and slowly incorporate the flour into the well. When all the flour is incorporated, begin to knead the dough with the base of your hands by pushing, rolling, and stretching the dough onto itself. The dough will look shaggy and dry until incorporated. If needed, add 1 or 2 tablespoons of additional water.

Transfer the dough to a clean, flat work surface dusted with flour and continue to knead for another 10 minutes or longer. If the dough is tough to knead, let it rest, covered with a clean kitchen towel, for 5 minutes. Eventually the dough will begin to feel smooth and silky, and there will be less resistance when the dough is ready. Tucking the dough underneath itself, form the dough into a smooth ball. Wrap the dough tightly with plastic wrap and let the dough rest, for 30 minutes.

Heat a medium heavy skillet over medium-low heat. Add a small amount of duck fat to the pan. Unwrap and divide the dough in half. Place half of the dough between 2 pieces of parchment paper. Roll the dough into a ⅛-inch-thick oblong disc, about 6 to 7½ inches long. Place the disc in the heated skillet and cook until freckled, about 1½ minutes. If it puffs, pierce the bubble(s) with a knife. Flip the dough with a spatula and cook the other side until freckled with some larger golden brown spots throughout, 1½ to 2 minutes. Repeat with the remaining half of dough. Piadina is best eaten the same day it's made, but once fully cooked, it can be wrapped in foil and refrigerated for 2 days. Warm the flatbread, wrapped in foil, in the oven before serving.

NOTE: Olive oil produces a stiffer dough than the duck fat, shortening, or lard, and the flatbread will be less pliable, so fold it over when still warm if using for a sandwich. If using olive oil, measure, freeze until solid, and then cut into small cubes before using. This slows the fat absorption into the flour.

SWEET BUTTERCREAM FROSTING

YIELD: About 2½ cups
PREP & COOK TIME: 30 minutes

USED IN: Rachel's Apple Chai Milk Tea Latte Cupcakes (page 167)

2 sticks unsalted butter, at room temperature
One 14-ounce can sweetened condensed milk, at room temperature

In the bowl of a stand mixer fitted with the whisk attachment, or in a medium bowl if using a handheld mixer, whisk the butter on medium-high until light and creamy. Whisk for a minimum of 10 minutes, stopping the mixer a few times to scrape down the sides and bottom of the bowl. Slowly add the condensed milk in ¼ cup additions and whisk until combined. Make sure the liquid is incorporated before adding more. If the buttercream looks watery, increase the speed to high and whisk until creamy before adding more condensed milk.

Buttercream can be made 1 week in advance and stored in a covered container in the refrigerator. Let the buttercream come to room temperature, then transfer it to the bowl of a stand mixer fitted with the paddle attachment and beat for 10 minutes, or until smooth. Switch to the whisk attachment and whisk until light and creamy, about 15 minutes.

Try this with chai flavoring, either store-bought or homemade (see Rachel's Apple Chai Milk Tea Latte Cupcakes, page 167). While whipping, slowly add 2 tablespoons of concentrate, 1 teaspoon at a time, making sure each addition is well incorporated before adding more.

BASIC GANACHE

YIELD: About 2¾ cups
PREP & COOK TIME: 10 minutes, plus time to cool

USED IN: Ross & Marcel's Famous Monkey Bars (page 159)

2 cups heavy cream
2 cups high-quality couverture baking chocolate, chopped, or 60% cacao chocolate chips

In a medium pot over medium heat, or in a heatproof pitcher in the microwave, heat the cream until it reads 185°F to 200°F on a quick-read thermometer. (If cream is heated over 200°F, the chocolate may break.)

Place the chocolate in a medium bowl. Pour the heated cream over the chocolate and wait a few minutes for the chocolate to begin melting, then stir mixture until smooth. Make sure no water comes into contact with the chocolate or it will seize.

TIP: The amount of cream may be adjusted slightly to either thin or thicken the ganache. For white chocolate, use a 2:1 or 3:1 chocolate-to-cream ratio.

NOTE: Confirm the type of chocolate and ratio of cream to chocolate for each recipe before making. In the United States, couverture chocolate must contain a minimum of 35% cocoa solids and 31% cocoa butter. It is best for tempering and decadent truffles. Baking chips with at least 60% cacao are fine for Ross & Marcel's Famous Monkey Bars (page 159) and Richard & Monica's Toasted Meringue "Mustache" S'mores Bars (page 163).

A MOO POINT

There is a science to getting the perfect milk consistency for a specialty drink, whether for a latte or a cappuccino.

It starts with the type of milk, temperature, and the equipment or tool used. For maximum sweetness, the milk temperature should be 140°F before pouring into any hot specialty drink. Not all milk will froth equally because fat content and protein affect the end results. Organic, lactose-free milk, and ultrapasteurized milk do not produce optimal results for latte art due to processing methods during production, but they will still work for a delicious home brew. Fresh milk that has been kept cold before frothing will provide the best results, although it's okay to warm up milk that has been sitting for a few seconds into order to perfectly time the pour into a pulled espresso.

* *Nonfat or skimmed milk* provide the largest foam or micro bubbles. This means they whip up fast but have less staying power.

* *Whole milk* produces the finest, richest tasting foam yet takes more finesse to achieve the ideal texture due to the extra fat in the milk.

* *Milk alternatives* don't hold up as well when frothed and are generally thinner. Also, milk proteins start to break down around 170°F and start scalding by 180°F, and plant and nut-milk proteins are different depending on the brand or type purchased. Practice frothing your favorite milk alternative to perfect the technique.

NUTTY MILK & FLAVORED MILKS

Nut milks are common milk alternatives made by soaking nuts in filtered water and blending at high speed until the mixture is creamy. Once strained, the nut milk lasts 2 to 3 days in the refrigerator. Combining oat milk or a nondairy coconut milk beverage with nuts after the nuts have been soaked (and before blending) instead of water adds more depth, complexity, and bold flavor for a smoother, more natural-tasting beverage. It's a great alternative to flavored syrups in coffee and tea drinks. This is just one perk of making coffee or tea drinks at home. The options and flavor combinations are endless.

HAZELNUT OAT MILK

YIELD: About 2 to 2½ cups (16 to 20 ounces)
PREP TIME: 8½ to 12 hours

USED IN: Rachel's Blackout Latte (page 61)

2 cups whole raw hazelnuts (or other nut, such as pecan), without skins if available
4 cups (32 ounces) cold filtered water, to soak nuts
3½ cups (28 ounces) filtered water, oat milk, or other milk alternative
1 to 2 teaspoons sweetener such as maple syrup, honey, sugar, or date syrup (optional)
Pinch of salt (optional)

Place the hazelnuts in a fine-mesh strainer and rinse under running water. Transfer the nuts to a large glass pitcher or bowl, add the cold water, and soak in the refrigerator for at least 8 hours, or up to 12 hours for larger nuts like pecans. Most nuts can soak for up to 48 hours to produce a more flavorful nut milk.

Strain the nuts and discard the soaking liquid. Rinse the nuts thoroughly. For hazelnuts, rub the nuts with a clean kitchen towel to remove any papery skin, if needed. Transfer the nuts and the 3½ cups of water to a blender or food processor. (A high-speed blender will provide more nut milk than a food processor.) Pulse until the nuts resemble a fine meal or, if using a high-speed blender, until the mixture looks creamy.

Place a nut-milk bag in a bowl or pitcher. Pour the nuts and milk into the nut-milk bag, or strain through a fine-mesh strainer lined with a filter, piece of muslin, or cheesecloth. Squeeze or press the liquid into the bowl or pitcher. Add the sweetener, if using, and salt, if using. Store in a covered sterile container in the refrigerator for up to 3 days.

Reserve the nut pulp for another use, such as the sweetened nut crumble recipe on Eddie's Angry Dried Fruit & Sweetened Nuts (page 100). If you want to freeze or dry the nuts, if using liquid other than water, thoroughly rinse the nut pulp several times before freezing or drying the nuts. Nut pulp can be frozen for several weeks before using, or dried out on a sheet tray in an oven set to low temperature (170°F to 200°F). Bake for 1 to 2 hours and stir the nut pulp every 30 minutes until dry but not colored or toasted. Let cool. Blend in a food processor and use in baked goods. Almond meal is used in Pete's Killer Financier Cakes (page 141).

NOTE: This recipe can be used with other nuts such as Brazil nuts, pecans, macadamias, pistachios, or cashews. Cashews and macadamia nuts are quick soaking and can be soaked for 2 hours; however, soaking longer creates a smoother milk. Rinse the nuts well before and after soaking, strain out the soaking water, and then add fresh water or milk alternative to the nuts before blending.

CEREAL & COOKIE MILK

Cookie or cereal milk is a delicious base for glazes or for specialty coffees, adding an extra layer of flavor. Experiment with different flavors for a specialty coffee or unique dessert topping. Sugary cereal blends add a bigger pop of flavor, although some natural oat, granola, or graham cracker cereals work well. Think of cinnamon-graham milk versus oat milk, or maybe a peanut butter cookie–flavored flat white, or vanilla wafer–flavored latte, or perhaps a fruit-cereal milk to top a cold brew foam. Be creative and try some new flavor combinations.

YIELD: About ½ cup (about 4 ounces)
PREP & COOK TIME: 15 minutes or overnight

USED IN: Ross's Cinnamon Toasty Fruit Tarts With Cereal Milk Icing (page 89), Gunther's Frosty Flakes Donuts With Cereal Milk Icing (page 135)

1 cup (8 ounces) milk or milk
    alternative
¾ cup crushed cereal or cookies

Cereal- and cookie-flavored milk can be made by warming the milk or cold steeping the milk with either cereal or cookies. The overnight steeping method will produce a more flavorful milk and is better for frothing than the quicker method of heating the milk and steeping the cereal or cookies.

QUICK METHOD: Warm the milk in a glass pitcher in a microwave, or in the barrel of an electric milk frother without the whisk attachment, for about 30 seconds. Stir in the crushed cereal and steep covered for 10 minutes. Strain and cool. Store in a covered container in the refrigerator for a minimum of 6 hours or overnight.

OVERNIGHT METHOD: To make cereal- or cookie-based milk for lattes or cappuccinos, steep the cereal or cookies in cold milk overnight and strain the milk before frothing. Some cookies or cereal will absorb more milk. Add additional milk if needed for a recipe. Heat the milk and froth for a signature flavored drink.

BASIC SWEET CREAM

YIELD: About 1 cup (8 ounces)
PREP & COOK TIME: 5 minutes, plus 24 hours if making coconut sweet cream

USED IN: Rachel's Vanilla Sweet Cream Cold Brew (page 67)

½ cup (4 ounces) heavy cream
1 tablespoon sweetened condensed milk
½ cup (4 ounces) half-and-half, nonfat milk, or milk alternative

FLAVORING OPTIONS
(choose one or a combination):
½ teaspoon Basic Simple Syrup (page 27)
2 teaspoons granulated sugar
1 tablespoon honey
1 tablespoon maple syrup
¼ teaspoon vanilla bean seeds or paste

Chill the cream, milk, and container used to make the sweet cream for 1 minute in the freezer. With an immersion blender, the whisk attachment, and a tall container, or in a medium bowl using a handheld mixer, whisk the cream until it begins to thicken, about 45 seconds. Add the condensed milk and whisk to incorporate, another 20 seconds. Whisk in ¼ cup of half-and-half until the mixture is foamy on top and looks like melted ice cream.

Add in the remaining ¼ cup of half-and-half, and whisk to combine. If using a flavoring, add the flavoring now and stir to combine.

COCONUT SWEET CREAM

½ cup full-fat coconut cream, chilled for 24 hours in the refrigerator
Pinch of baking soda
½ teaspoon coconut extract (optional)

To make coconut sweet cream, follow the instructions for basic sweet cream above, but replace the heavy cream with full-fat coconut cream or use a milk alternative, preferably a nondairy coconut beverage. Add the baking soda and coconut extract, if using, with the last addition of coconut cream. Continue whisking to combine.

NOTE: Plan ahead as coconut cream will need to be refrigerated for at least 24 hours before using. Either buy a can of 100 percent coconut cream or full-fat coconut milk and chill the can. For coconut milk, open the can from the bottom. Pour out any coconut liquid and scoop out the cream only. Coconut cream will not have any coconut liquid. Lite coconut milk will not whip and will not work for this recipe. If using a milk alternative, use a nondairy coconut milk beverage (in the carton), not straight coconut milk from a can.

BASIC CHEESE FOAM

YIELD: About ½ cup
PREP & COOK TIME: 10 minutes

USED IN: Rachel's Matcha Salted "Tears" Macchiato (page 64)

3 tablespoons cream cheese, at room temperature

3 tablespoons heavy cream, at room temperature

1 to 2 tablespoons granulated sugar

¼ cup milk or half-and-half, at room temperature

Pinch of baking soda

Pinch of salt (optional)

In a medium bowl or tall container, using a handheld mixer or immersion blender with a whisk attachment, blend the cream cheese and heavy cream until thoroughly combined, smooth, and lump-free, 1 to 2 minutes. (It's important that the ingredients are at room temperature, so that lumps do not form and it will be easier to blend.) Add the sugar and blend until combined, about 1 to 2 minutes. Slowly add in the milk, whisking in between additions. Whisk in the baking soda. The mixture can be stored in a covered container in the refrigerator for up to 1 day. Whisk again just before serving. Sprinkle salt, if using, on top or whisk into the cheese foam for an added flavor enhancer.

> **TIP:** Use dark brown sugar, honey powder, maple powder, or maple syrup for a unique flavor combination. Use a 1:1 substitution in the recipe, or adjust to your desired level of sweetness.

HONEY CHEESE FOAM

To make honey cheese foam, swap the granulated sugar for 1 to 2 tablespoons of honey in the recipe.

WHIPPED CREAM

YIELD: About 2 cups
PREP & COOK TIME: 15 minutes

USED IN: Monica's Whipped-Up Pumpkin Spiced Latte (page 45), Phoebe's Apple Chai Milk Tea Latte (page 49), Chandler's Better Than "Nubbin" Fiery Gingerbread Latte (page 57), Phoebe's Jingle Thief Cappuccino With Peppermint Milk Foam (page 63), Phoebe's Chocolate Espresso "Mugged" Cake (page 145), Rachel's Apple Chai Milk Tea Latte Cupcakes (page 167)

1 cup heavy cream, very cold, plus more as needed
2 tablespoons granulated sugar or powdered sugar

Chill a medium stainless steel or glass bowl. Place the cream in the chilled bowl and whisk until soft peaks form, 3 to 5 minues. Add the sugar and whisk until the cream is dense and billowy with firm peaks, 3 to 5 minutes. If using an immersion blender with a whisk attachment, proceed with directions, but use the tall plastic container (chilled) that comes with the blender to whisk the ingredients. If the cream is overwhisked, it will look chunky and thick. Stir in a small amount of cream until the texture is creamy again. This trick only works if the cream is not whipped to the "almost-butter" stage! The whipped cream can be made 1 day in advance and stored in a covered container in the refrigerator. Whisk the cream for a few seconds before using.

FOR COCONUT WHIPPED CREAM: Add 1 teaspoon of coconut extract to the basic Whipped Cream recipe for coconut-flavored whipped cream or use coconut cream for a nondairy option. See note on page 33 for tips.

CARAMEL FILLING

YIELD: About 2 cups
PREP & COOK TIME: 25 minutes

USED IN: Ross & Marcel's Famous Monkey Bars (page 159), Richard & Monica's Toasted Meringue "Mustache" S'mores Bars (page 163)

3 tablespoons unsalted butter
One 14-ounce can sweetened condensed milk
2 tablespoons golden syrup
⅛ teaspoons salt

In a medium saucepan over medium-high heat, combine the butter, condensed milk, and golden syrup. Whisk rapidly while cooking until the mixture thickens and begins to change to a light caramel color, about 10 minutes. Whisk in the salt. Use right away while hot.

Sips

AND

Brews

CHANDLER'S DETOX JUICE

SEASON 4, EP: 15

"The One With All the Rugby"

One of Chandler's on-again, off-again girlfriends is loud and over-the-top Janice, who has an unforgettable laugh. Nobody in the group really likes her, except for Chandler, and even he doesn't seem to like her all that much. Chandler tries to break up with Janice multiple times, and in one scenario, creates a fanciful story about leaving the country for Yemen just to escape their relationship. Maybe if he'd had this juice, he would have had an easier time detoxing from Janice.

DIFFICULTY: Easy
YIELD: 1 serving, ¾ to 1 cup (6 to 8 ounces)
PREP & COOK TIME: 15 minutes

1 medium green apple, cored
½ medium cucumber, peeled
2-inch piece fresh ginger,
   peeled and grated
2 cups baby spinach
Juice of 1 lemon
Juice of 1 orange
Pinch of cayenne pepper (optional)

Slice the apple and the cucumber into pieces that will fit into the juicer's feed tube. Place an appropriate size glass under the spout. Turn on the juicer and add the apple and ginger to the feed tube, then the cucumber and spinach. Add the lemon juice and orange juice directly to the glass. Stir and add the cayenne, if using. Enjoy at room temperature or over ice.

NOTE: Grate the ginger before adding to the feed tube as a small piece of ginger may not break down in the juicer. If using a professional blender instead of a juicer, mince the ginger and add to the barrel with the other ingredients. Strain before serving, if desired.

"CHANDLER, COME ON.
I'M GOING TO SHOW YOU HOW TO ROLL UP YOUR UNDERWEAR AND STUFF IT IN YOUR SHOES. IT'S A REAL SPACE SAVER."

Janice

MONICA'S "MOCKOLATE" PEANUT BUTTER COOKIE AND CARAMEL BLENDED SHAKE

When Monica takes a new job developing recipes, one of her tasks is to create Mockolate, a synthetic chocolate substitute. The fake chocolate tastes so bad that her only option is to drastically increase the other ingredients in the recipe to make it palatable. You won't have that problem with this delicious peanut butter cookie and caramel shake!

DIFFICULTY: Easy
YIELD: 1 to 2 servings, 2¼ cups (18 ounces)
PREP & COOK TIME: 10 minutes

1 cup Dutch chocolate ice cream

1 cup vanilla ice cream

4 store-bought peanut butter cookies, crushed

¼ cup (2 ounces) half-and-half

2 tablespoons malted milk powder (optional)

¼ cup Whipped Cream (page 35)

1 tablespoon Salted Caramel Sauce (page 26) or salted caramel with espresso powder

1 tablespoon crushed raw or roasted salted peanuts

In a blender, blend the chocolate and vanilla ice creams, cookies, and half-and-half until smooth and creamy. Blend in the malted milk powder, if using.

To serve the shake, pour it into a tall glass, top with the whipped cream, and drizzle with the caramel sauce and peanuts.

> "I LOVE MOCKOLATE!
> ESPECIALLY THAT AFTERTASTE.
> I TELL YOU, THAT'LL LAST YOU
> 'TIL CHRISTMAS."
>
> Monica

PHOEBE'S UBE COCONUT LATTE MACCHIATO

Phoebe Buffay, Regina Phalange. What's in a name? Phoebe is unabashedly wacky and one of a kind, as is this beautiful purple latte macchiato that uses a purple sweet potato called ube, which kind of rhymes with Buffay, if you think about it. We think Phoebe would be so tickled by that she might even write a song about ube.

DIFFICULTY: Easy
YIELD: 1 serving, 1 cup (8 ounces)
PREP & COOK TIME: 30 minutes

FOR THE UBE BASE:

1 medium ube or purple sweet
    potato
1 tablespoon sweetened
    condensed coconut milk
½ cup (4 ounces) full-fat or lite
    coconut milk

FOR THE MACCHIATO:

½ to ¾ cup (2 to 6 ounces) dairy-
    free coconut milk beverage
⅛ teaspoon Lavender Vanilla
    Simple Syrup (page 47)
    (optional)

FUN FACT: *Macchiato* in Italian translates to "stained," which is why it has a signature dot on top.

TO MAKE THE UBE BASE: Peel and dice the ube. Prepare a pot with a steamer. Add water to the pot and bring to a boil. Add the ube and steam, covered, until fork-tender, 10 to 15 minutes.

In a bowl, mash the cooked ube with a fork.

In a small bowl, using a handheld mixer or an immersion blender, combine the mashed ube with the sweetened condensed coconut milk. Slowly incorporate the coconut milk until fully combined. For a smoother texture, pass the mixture through a strainer by pushing it through the strainer with a spatula into a clean bowl. Set aside. Warm in a microwave-safe bowl in the microwave for about 40 seconds just before making the macchiato

TO MAKE THE MACCHIATO: Reserve 2 tablespoons of ube base and set aside. Froth the coconut milk beverage for a latte (see page 11 for instructions). Heat the milk until the temperature reaches 140°F on an instant-read thermometer for maximum flavor. If the milk is not the correct temperature, warm the milk, whisk some more, and swirl and tap the frothing container on the counter to remove any large bubbles. This action creates a finer microfoam. Stir the reserved ube into the frothed milk. Pour over the warm ube base, reserving a small amount of frothed milk for the heart on top. Pour the remaining frothed milk over the ube down the center of the latte to create a small 1-inch dot on the foam. Run a knife through the center of the dot and down to create a heart shape.

For an extra-sweet treat, add the lavender vanilla syrup to the frothed milk. Enjoy!

NOTE: While not the same thing, purple Japanese sweet potatoes or yams can be substituted for ube if you cannot find ube. A drop of ube paste (purchased online) can be added to the coconut milk for a stronger ube flavor.

JOEY'S LONDON-STYLE STRAWBERRY SMOOTHIE

SEASON 4, EP: 23-24

"The One With Ross's Wedding"

Unlike Ross, who often seems to be a bit clueless when it comes to women, Joey is always so smooth. While in foggy London for Ross and Emily's wedding, Joey hooks up with Felicity, one of Emily's bridesmaids, who feeds him strawberries in the bathtub. In honor of that steamy moment, and the cool weather of London, this refreshing smoothie would surely remind Joey of the exciting encounter.

DIFFICULTY: Easy
YIELD: 1 serving, 1½ cups (12 ounces)
PREP & COOK TIME: 10 minutes, plus 4 to 6 hours to freeze ice

2 Earl Grey tea bags
1 cup fresh, or slightly thawed frozen strawberries, hulled
½ cup plain kefir
1 to 2 tablespoons honey
2 Medjool dates, seeded and chopped
¼ cup whipped Coconut Sweet Cream (page 33) or Whipped Cream (page 35) (optional)

In a small saucepan over medium heat, bring ¾ cup of water to a simmer. Remove from the heat and steep the tea bags in the hot water for 2 minutes. Remove the tea bags and let the tea cool. Pour into ice cube trays and freeze until solid, about 4 to 6 hours.

In a blender, purée the strawberries, kefir, honey, and dates until almost smooth. Add the frozen tea cubes and blend until very smooth and creamy. Taste and adjust sweetness with more honey if desired.

To serve, pour or spoon the smoothie into a glass and top with the coconut sweet cream, if using.

MONICA'S WHIPPED-UP PUMPKIN SPICED LATTE

SEASON 7, EP: 9

"The One With All the Candy"

This sweet, whipped pumpkin spice and coffee-flavored treat, inspired by a Dalgona candy, is like "little drops of heaven." We can just imagine Monica whipping up this delicious holiday-themed brew with the same energy she puts into making holiday candy for all the neighbors. As Monica said, "Love it!"

DIFFICULTY: Medium
YIELD: 1 serving, 1 cup (8 ounces)
PREP & COOK TIME: 12 minutes

FOR THE WHIPPED COFFEE:
2 tablespoons instant coffee or espresso powder
2 tablespoons maple sugar granules
2 tablespoons hot water (95°F)

FOR THE SPICED MILK:
½ to ¾ cup (4 to 6 ounces) milk
¼ teaspoon pumpkin pie spice
½ teaspoon vanilla extract
Ice (optional)

FOR SERVING:
2 tablespoons Whipped Cream (page 35) or straight cream
Pinch of fine sea or table salt

TO MAKE THE WHIPPED COFFEE: In a medium bowl with a handheld blender, whisk the instant coffee, maple sugar granules, and hot water on high speed until light and airy, about 10 minutes. Alternatively, use an immersion blender with a whisk attachment and a tall container to whisk the ingredients, 3 to 5 minutes.

TO MAKE THE SPICED MILK: In a small saucepan over medium-low heat, warm the milk, 2 teaspoons of whipped coffee, the pumpkin pie spice, and vanilla. Prepare the spiced milk for a latte or cappuccino (see page 11 for instructions). Heat the spiced milk until the temperature reaches 140°F on an instant-read thermometer. If the spiced milk is not the correct temperature, warm the milk, whisk some more, and swirl and tap the frothing container on the counter to remove any large bubbles. This action creates a finer microfoam. Pour the frothed spiced milk into a mug. Alternatively, if making a cold drink, add ice to a glass and pour the spiced milk on top.

TO SERVE: Spoon the remaining whipped coffee on top of the spiced milk. Top with the whipped cream and a sprinkle of salt.

PHOEBE'S GURU SAJ SPICY MANGO LASSI OF LOVE

When Phoebe sends Ross to her herbalist for the weird thing on his back, the herbalist tells Ross to "love the Koondis." Instead, he accidentally removes it with his watch! Maybe it's a sign to take time with things you love, and Ross could start with this mango lassi.

DIFFICULTY: Easy
YIELD: 1 serving, 1 cup (8 ounces)
COOK & PREP TIME: 15 minutes, plus 15 minutes to chill mango

FOR THE SYRUP:
1-inch piece fresh ginger, peeled and sliced
2 tablespoons granulated sugar
3 tablespoons water
Pinch of cayenne pepper

FOR THE LASSI:
1 cup ripe fresh mango, chopped, or mango purée (if frozen, slightly defrost the mango)
¾ cup whole-milk yogurt
1 to 2 tablespoons milk
Pinch of cayenne pepper, for garnish
⅛ teaspoon ground cardamom, for garnish
1 lime wedge

TO MAKE THE SYRUP: In a small saucepan over medium heat, combine the ginger, sugar, water, and cayenne and stir until the sugar is dissolved, 1 to 2 minutes. Remove from the heat and let cool. The syrup can be made 1 day in advance and stored in a covered container in the refrigerator. If the syrup is very thick, thin out with a teaspoon or two of water before using.

TO MAKE THE LASSI: Place the mango in the freezer for about 15 minutes, or until hard but not frozen solid. Add the chilled mango to a food processor, or use an immersion blender, and blend until smooth.

Reserve the ginger pieces in the syrup for a garnish. Add 1 tablespoon of spicy ginger simple syrup, the yogurt, and milk to the puréed mango and pulse until smooth. If the mango is not fully ripe, the purée may not be completely smooth; you can run it through a strainer if desired.

Pour the lassi into a glass. Before serving, drizzle the remaining ginger syrup on top of the drink. Garnish with the reserved ginger, the cayenne, and cardamom. Add the wedge of lime before serving. The lassi can be covered and refrigerated for a couple days after blending. Garnish just before serving.

TIP: To peel the ginger, use the edge of a teaspoon to scrape and peel off the outer skin before slicing.

"WOAH! CLEARLY, NOT THE WAY TO GO . . . WE APPEARED TO HAVE ANGERED IT."

Guru Saj

CHANDLER'S LAVENDER PEPPERMINT TEA LATTE

SEASON 8, EP: 13

"The One Where Chandler Takes a Bath, Part 1"

In an effort to help Chandler relax, Monica convinces him to take a bubble bath, complete with bath salts and candles. She even buys him a battleship to give the bath a more masculine feel. Next on the checklist, a soothing, peppermint tea latte. If only Monica's massages were this soothing. Ouch!

DIFFICULTY: Easy
YIELD: 1 serving, 1 cup (8 ounces)
PREP & COOK TIME: 10 minutes, plus overnight for lavender milk

FOR THE LAVENDER MILK:
½ cup (4 ounces) milk
½ teaspoon dried culinary lavender

FOR THE LAVENDER VANILLA SIMPLE SYRUP:
¼ cup (2 ounces) water
¼ cup granulated sugar
¼ vanilla bean pod, sliced open
1 teaspoon dried culinary lavender

FOR THE TEA:
1 cup (8 ounces) water
1 peppermint tea bag

TO MAKE THE LAVENDER MILK: Place the milk in a mug or small bowl. Put the culinary lavender in a tea ball and submerge the ball in the milk. Cover and refrigerate overnight.

TO MAKE THE LAVENDER VANILLA SIMPLE SYRUP: In a small saucepan over medium heat, bring the water, sugar, and vanilla to a boil. Remove from the heat. Add the culinary lavender and steep, covered, for 5 minutes. Strain the mixture and let cool. The syrup can be stored in a covered container in the refrigerator for up to 5 days. Use a small amount of water to thin if needed.

TO MAKE THE TEA: In a tea kettle, microwave, or a small saucepan, bring the water to a boil. Place the tea bag in a mug. Pour the boiling water into the mug and let steep, covered, for 3 minutes. Remove the tea bag.

While tea is brewing, remove the lavender from the milk. Froth the lavender milk for a latte (see page 11 for instructions). Heat the milk until the temperature reaches 140°F on an instant-read thermometer for maximum flavor. If the milk is not the correct temperature, warm the milk, whisk some more, and swirl and tap the frothing container on the counter to remove any large bubbles. This action creates a finer microfoam. Add 1 teaspoon of lavender vanilla simple syrup to the milk. Taste and add more lavender syrup if desired, or drizzle additional syrup on top before serving. Pour the milk over the tea and enjoy! Bubble bath and battleship are optional.

> "OH. THE BATH SALTS. THEY'RE STARTING TO EFFERVESCE. IT'S DIFFERENT. IT'S INTERESTING."
> Chandler

MONICA'S "I'M NOT SICK!" IMMUNITY BOOSTER

SEASON 6, EP: 13

"The One With Rachel's Sister"

When Monica gets sick, she refuses to admit it. Instead, she tries to convince Chandler to fool around with her, but he is grossed out until she convinces him to rub her down with Vicks VapoRub. Maybe if she'd had this tasty immunity booster drink, she would have been well enough to fool around. Fresh fruit is fine to use in this recipe; however, to create the right consistency, it's recommended that at least two of the fruits listed below are used frozen. The remaining fruit can be fresh or frozen, depending on what is in season.

DIFFICULTY: Easy
YIELD: 2 servings, About 2½ cups (20 ounces)
PREP & COOK TIME: 10 minutes, plus 4 hours to freeze fruit if needed

Juice of 1 lime
1 tablespoon chia seeds
1½ cups fresh cubed pineapple
½ medium green apple, cored and diced
1 small to medium cubed red dragon fruit (1 cup)
½ cup cubed mango
3 Medjool dates, seeded and chopped
¼ cup unsweetened coconut water

In a small bowl, combine the lime juice and chia seeds. Let the seeds rehydrate for 10 minutes. Set aside.

Place the pineapple, apple, and dragon fruit in a blender or food processor and blend until smooth. Add the mango and dates and blend or pulse until incorporated. Add the coconut water and the chia and lime mixture and blend until smooth.

For a sweeter drink, add additional dates, a few strawberries, or juice such as pineapple, orange, or tangerine.

NOTE: Red dragon fruit, also called pitaya, is high in vitamin C and tastes like a cross between kiwi and pear. The seeds inside the fruit are edible. It can be found in the freezer section of well-stocked supermarkets in cubes or in unsweetened smoothie packets. If using 3.5-ounce smoothie packets, use two in the recipe. Fresh pitaya can also be scooped out of the fruit, diced, and frozen.

> ## "ARE YOU SAYING THAT YOU DON'T WANNA GET WITH THIS?"
> Monica

PHOEBE'S APPLE CHAI MILK TEA LATTE

Phoebe is a rare mix of sweet and spice and not the all-American girl Mike's parents were hoping their son would date. After fashion tips and lessons from Rachel on how to please Mike's elitist parents, Phoebe takes her role a bit over the edge with a Kennedy-esque accent and bizarre antics to impress them. Phoebe may not feel like she fits in with Mike's parents, but Mike's still a fan. Like Phoebe, who says apple pie has to be boring or basic? This latte certainly isn't! It's rich and creamy with the perfect amount spice.

DIFFICULTY: Easy
YIELD: 1 serving, 1 cup (8 ounces)
PREP & COOK TIME: 15 minutes, plus overnight to steep spiced milk

FOR THE SPICED CARAMEL SAUCE:
Pinch of ground cinnamon
Pinch of freshly grated nutmeg
Salted Caramel Sauce (page 26),
    freshly made and hot

FOR THE CHAI SPICED MILK:
½ cup (4 ounces) milk
1 cinnamon stick
One 2-inch strip orange peel
¼- to ½-inch piece fresh ginger, peeled
    and thinly sliced
3 whole cardamom pods, crushed
1 star anise pod
½ tablespoon Chai Spice Mix (page 167),
    (optional)

FOR THE BLACK TEA:
¼ cup (2 ounces) water
1 black tea bag, or 1¼ teaspoons loose
    (Tetley brand)

FOR THE LATTE:
2 teaspoons granulated sugar, or 1½
    tablespoons honey
Single shot espresso (optional)
¼ to ½ cup Whipped Cream (page 35)
Cinnamon stick, for garnish (optional)
Dried or freeze-dried apple slice, for
    garnish (optional)

TO MAKE THE SPICED CARAMEL SAUCE: Add the cinnamon and nutmeg to the caramel. Stir to combine. When ready to use, warm on the stove over low heat or in the microwave for 15 seconds.

TO MAKE THE CHAI SPICED MILK: In a glass measuring pitcher, combine the milk, cinnamon stick, orange peel, ginger, cardamom, and star anise and let steep overnight. Strain. Alternatively, use only the spice mix and orange peel.

TO MAKE THE BLACK TEA: In a microwave, tea kettle, or small saucepan, boil the water. Pour into a mug, submerge the tea bag (or tea ball with loose leaves), and steep, covered, for 4 minutes.

TO MAKE THE LATTE: Froth the chai spiced milk for a latte (see instructions on page 11). Heat the milk until the temperature reaches 140°F on an instant-read thermometer for maximum flavor. If the milk is not the correct temperature, warm the milk, whisk some more, and swirl and tap the frothing container on the counter to remove any large bubbles. This action creates a finer microfoam. Add the sugar to sweeten the milk or stir into the hot tea. Reheat or froth the milk as needed to maintain the proper texture and temperature. Add the espresso, if using, to the tea. Add the spiced milk. Top with the whipped cream. Garnish with the cinnamon stick and/or apple slice, if using. Yum!

RACHEL'S SANGRIA PASSION FRUIT TEA

SEASON 7, EP: 20

"The One With Rachel's Big Kiss"

Rachel's old sorority sister, Melissa, shows up at Central Perk one day, and the two are delighted to catch up. Rachel confesses to Phoebe that she had a clandestine kiss with Melissa in college after too much sangria. Phoebe doesn't believe Rachel, stating that Rachel doesn't do crazy things because she is just too "vanilla." This sangria, with a hint of vanilla, is so delicious it's sure to leave a lasting impression, just like the one Rachel left on Melissa. Serve with or without the optional brewed tea.

DIFFICULTY: Easy
YIELD: 2 servings, About 2 to 2¼ cup (16 to 18 ounces)
PREP & COOK TIME: 15 minutes, plus 1 hour to chill

2 whole passion fruits, fresh, pulp and seeds scooped out and flesh discarded (or 1 tablespoon juice with seeds or frozen passion fruit puree)
1 cup (8 ounces) white grape juice
¼ cup (2 ounces) sparkling apple juice
Juice of ½ large orange
Juice of ½ medium lemon
Juice of ½ lime
½ medium Fuji or Honey Crisp apple, cored and diced
½ orange, unpeeled, sliced, and quartered
½ lime, sliced
½ lemon, sliced and halved
¼-inch piece vanilla bean (optional)
½ cup (4 ounces) brewed vanilla or passion fruit tea, cooled (optional)

In a glass pitcher, stir together the passion fruit pulp and seeds, if using, grape juice, apple juice, orange juice, lemon juice, lime juice, apple, orange, lime, lemon, and vanilla, if using. Refrigerate for 1 hour, or until chilled. Add some ice and use a slotted spoon to add some of the cut fruit from the fruit sangria to each glass just before serving. Pour ¼ cup of tea, if using, in each glass, then pour the fruit sangria into each glass. Spoon any remaining fruit into each glass. Serve with a long teaspoon on the side.

TIP: If fresh passion fruit or frozen passion fruit purée is not available, substitute mango purée or blended fresh kiwi.

"IT WAS SENIOR YEAR IN COLLEGE . . .
AND MELISSA AND I GOT VERY DRUNK,
AND WE ENDED UP KISSING . . .
FOR SEVERAL MINUTES."

Rachel

JULIE'S HONG KONG MILK TEA WITH BOBA

SEASON 2, EP: 1

"The One With Ross's New Girlfriend"

Ross meets one of his girlfriends, Julie, while on a business trip to China. However, things aren't as perfect as he thought when he realizes he still has feelings for Rachel. A popular beverage in Hong Kong, this sweetened milk and black tea drink with tapioca pearls is also known as bubble tea. It's refreshing with the right amount of sweet and chewy tapioca pearls. This drink can be served either hot or cold, which seems to mirror Ross and Julie's relationship.

DIFFICULTY: Hard
YIELD: 2 servings, two 7-ounce hot, or 10-ounce cold
PREP & COOK TIME: 35 minutes, plus 35 minutes for boba, if using

HOT MILK TEA

3½ cups (28 ounces) water
3 black tea bags (Tetly brand)
2 black tea bags (Lipton brand)
2 tablespoons sweetened condensed milk
1 cup (8 ounces) evaporated milk
1 teaspoon honey
1 teaspoon granulated sugar

ICED TEA WITH BOBA (OPTIONAL)

1 cup boba
½ cup (4 ounces) Basic Simple Syrup made with honey or brown sugar (page 27)
1 cup ice cubes
¼ cup (2 ounces) half-and-half

TO MAKE THE HOT MILK TEA: In a kettle or medium saucepan, heat the water over medium-high heat. Add the tea bags to the water and bring to a boil. When the tea begins to foam, turn the heat to low. Cover and continue heating for 5 minutes.

Remove the saucepan from the heat, discard the tea bags, and pour the tea through a fine-mesh strainer into a heatproof pitcher. Aerate the tea by pouring it from a height of 10 inches back into the kettle or saucepan used to make the tea. Repeat the action of aerating the tea 4 to 6 times with the tea ending up in the saucepan on the last pour. Return the tea to the stovetop and heat on low until ready to pour.

Divide the condensed milk, evaporated milk, honey, and sugar evenly between two mugs and stir to combine. Pour slightly less than 1 cup of hot tea into each mug. Stir and enjoy, or make iced boba tea.

FOR ICED BOBA TEA: Chill the milk tea in the refrigerator. The milk tea can be made 1 day in advance and, once cooled, stored in a glass container in the refrigerator.

Prepare the boba according to package instructions. Make sure the boba is not crowded and there is plenty of water in the pot. Stir frequently to prevent sticking.

Place the simple syrup in a bowl or a pitcher. Strain the cooked boba. Add the strained boba to the simple syrup. Chill in the refrigerator before using. For the characteristic chewy texture, it needs to be consumed within 24 hours of preparing.

To make boba milk tea, set up 2 tall glasses. Add the boba and about 2 tablespoons of syrup to each glass. Add ice as desired and the cold milk tea. Top each glass with the half-and-half and, for a sweeter drink, pour any remaining syrup on top. Add an extra-large straw, to enjoy the boba, or serve with a long iced-tea spoon.

MR. GELLER HAUTE HAVANA CAFÉ

Phoebe is smitten with Mr. Geller after she has a wacky dream in which he saves her from a fire. She even thinks it's alluring when she notices him chugging a can of sweetened condensed milk after the friends' Thanksgiving dinner. Maybe it would have been better if Mr. Geller had been drinking this popular sweet Cuban coffee drink, which features condensed milk, instead.

This drink has a strong coffee flavor with a creamy caramel sugar layer on top. The caramel layer on top, called *espumita*, is the perfect complement to the traditionally bitter overtones in this brew. For an authentic drink, invest in or borrow a stovetop brewer and use demerara sugar for a deep, rich caramel flavor. The sugar paste can be layered over a double espresso; however, it doesn't have the same balance of flavor as achieved with a stovetop brewer. This specialty coffee takes a little extra effort to make, just like one of Monica's Thanksgiving dinners, but the end result is worth it!

DIFFICULTY: Hard
YIELD: 6 demitasse servings
PREP & COOK TIME: 15 minutes

3 to 4 tablespoons medium-fine ground espresso roast coffee
Pinch of cayenne pepper (optional)
⅛ teaspoon ground cinnamon
3 to 4 tablespoons demerara or granulated sugar, plus more as desired
Pinch of salt (optional)
Heavy cream or condensed milk, for serving

Fill the chamber of a 6-cup stovetop espresso brewer with water and fill the filter with the ground coffee. Place the pot on the stove and start brewing with the lid open.

To make the *espumita*, combine the cayenne, if using, with the cinnamon, 3 tablespoons of sugar, and the salt, if using, in a small metal or glass pitcher. Set aside.

When the espresso has brewed, pour a couple drops of espresso at a time into the pitcher with the sugar and cinnamon to create the *espumita*. Whisk or stir the cinnamon-sugar mixture vigorously until the liquid is absorbed and the sugar crystals start to melt. Continue to add more drops of brewed coffee, a couple at a time, and continue to whisk or stir vigorously. The ratio of sugar and coffee is perfected when the mixture is thick and pasty with pale caramel tones and some noticeable grains of sugar (if using demerara sugar) or a smoother texture (if using granulated sugar). Be careful not to add too much liquid at once, because the paste won't form. The sugar can't be overwhipped, so strive for a good arm workout.

In the meantime, place the coffee maker back on the stovetop over medium heat and finish brewing. When ready, pour the heavy sugar paste in the top of the pot over the coffee and spoon in any remaining sugar paste. Most of the sugar will settle on the top and create a layer of thick foamy *espumita*.

Pour the coffee into individual demitasse cups and serve with cream or condensed milk on the side and a demitasse spoon. Delicioso!

TIP: After serving the coffee, pour some water in the top of the stovetop brewer to prevent any residual sugar from hardening. For best results, make this recipe with Cuban coffee and a fine grind between pour over and espresso. For a sweeter brew, add more sugar while making the sugar paste.

"I HAD A DREAM ABOUT MR. GELLER LAST NIGHT . . . I DREAMT HE SAVED ME FROM A BURNING BUILDING. HE WAS SO BRAVE AND SO STRONG. AND IT'S MAKING ME LOOK AT HIM TOTALLY DIFFERENTLY. . . NOW HE IS JACK GELLER: DREAM HUNK . . . OH, RACHEL, LOOK AT HIM, LOOK AT THOSE STRONG HANDS. WHAT I WOULDN'T GIVE TO BE THAT CAN OF CONDENSED MILK."

Phoebe

CHANDLER'S BETTER THAN "NUBBIN" FIERY GINGERBREAD LATTE

Joey panics when he sees Ginger, Chandler's new romantic interest, because he used to date her. In fact, things didn't end well when he accidentally threw her wooden leg into the lit fireplace during a woodsy cabin getaway. Meanwhile, Chandler grapples with dating Ginger, because of her wooden leg and his rather regrettable quest to find the "perfect" woman. In a curious twist of fate, Ginger rejects Chandler because of his "nubbin." In honor of Ginger, Chandler, and the fiery incident, make this delicious gingerbread latte, perfect for your own woodsy getaway.

DIFFICULTY: Easy
YIELD: 1 serving, 1 cup (8 ounces)
PREP & COOK TIME: 15 minutes

FOR THE GINGERBREAD SYRUP:

3 tablespoons plus ¼ teaspoon light or dark brown sugar
1 tablespoon granulated sugar
1-inch piece fresh ginger, peeled and thinly sliced
Pinch of ground allspice
Pinch of ground cardamom
Pinch of cayenne pepper, plus more for extra heat
⅛ teaspoon ground white pepper
Pinch of freshly grated nutmeg
¼ cup (2 ounces) water
1 teaspoon molasses
1 cinnamon stick, or ½ teaspoon ground cinnamon

FOR THE GINGERBREAD LATTE:

½ to ¾ cup (4 to 6 ounces) milk of choice
Double shot espresso
¼ cup Whipped Cream (page 35)
Freshly grated nutmeg, for garnish
Pinch of cayenne pepper, for garnish
Pinch of ground cinnamon, for garnish

TO MAKE THE GINGERBREAD SYRUP: In a small nonstick saucepan over medium heat, add the brown sugar, granulated sugar, ginger, allspice, cardamom, cayenne, white pepper, nutmeg, water, molasses, and cinnamon and stir to combine. Cook without stirring until the surface is coated with bubbles, about 3 minutes. Remove from the heat and stir. Return the pan to the heat and heat the syrup until bubbles form on the surface, about 30 seconds, and then remove the pan from the heat. Repeat this step two times. Remove the syrup from the heat. Cover and let steep 10 minutes. Strain the syrup into a heatproof pitcher or bowl and let cool. The syrup will thicken as it cools. The syrup can be made in advance and stored, once cool, in a covered container in the refrigerator for up to 3 days. Add a teaspoon of warm water if needed to thin syrup before using.

TO MAKE THE GINGERBREAD LATTE: Put 2 tablespoons of gingerbread syrup in a mug. Prepare the milk for a latte (see page 11 for instructions). Heat the milk until the temperature reaches 140°F on an instant-read thermometer. If the milk is not the correct temperature, warm the milk, whisk some more, and swirl and tap the frothing container on the counter to remove any large bubbles. This action creates a finer microfoam. Separately pull two espressos into the syrup and stir to combine. Pour the milk into the espresso and syrup. Spoon or pipe the whipped cream on top. Add the nutmeg, cayenne, and cinnamon. For a sweeter and spicer latte, drizzle the remaining gingerbread syrup on top.

PHOEBE'S BLUE BUTTERFLY PEA FLOWER TEA LEMONADE

This lemonade, which shifts color from blue to lavender after the lemonade is added, symbolizes Phoebe's transformation into a new bride and highlights her being the "something blue" at her wedding. Phoebe isn't going to let a blizzard ruin her wedding day! She's willing to freeze in order to marry the love of her life, Mike Hannigan. Instead of the formal wedding they'd planned, the couple gets married in the snow in front of Central Perk. The big wedding day is chaotic, but this iced tea is sure to create a tasty Zen mood.

DIFFICULTY: Easy
YIELD: 1 serving, 1 cup (8 ounces)
PREP & COOK TIME: 10 minutes

¾ cup (6 ounces) water
6 dried blue butterfly pea flowers (purchased online or at specialty markets)
5 to 6 tablespoons granulated sugar, divided
¼ cup (2 ounces) lemon juice
Ice, for serving
Sliced lemon or orange, for garnish

> **TIP:** To get more juice from the lemons, press and roll them on a hard surface with the palm of your hand for several seconds before juicing.

In a small saucepan over high heat, bring the water to a boil. Remove from the heat, add the dried pea flowers, and steep for 5 minutes. Let cool.

In a small bowl, mix 1 tablespoon of sugar with the lemon juice. Add 1 additional tablespoon sugar, if desired.

To sugar the glass rim, spread the remaining 3 to 4 tablespoons of sugar on a small plate. Dip the rim of glass into the lemonade base and then into the sugar. Add ice to the glass. Pour the tea into the glass. Pour the lemonade base on top of the tea. Watch the tea color change from blue to purple. Add the orange to the rim of the glass and serve.

"I'LL BE MY SOMETHING BLUE."
Phoebe

I HATE RACHEL THAI ICED TEA

Ross's friend Will really hated Rachel in high school because he had a crush on her and she didn't pay him any attention, so he started the I Hate Rachel Club. The club had three members: Ross, Will, and a foreign-exchange student from Thailand. In honor of the club, this Thai iced tea, with the traditional dark orange color, a hint of vanilla, and creamy half-and-half, is just one way to get Rachel's attention. We recommend using Wangderm tea for this recipe because it provides the most traditional Thai iced tea flavor.

DIFFICULTY: Easy
YIELD: 1 serving, 1½ cups (12 ounces)
PREP & COOK TIME: 5 minutes, plus time to chill tea

¾ cup (6 ounces) water
1 Thai-flavored tea bag (Wangderm brand)
3 tablespoons sweetened condensed milk or sweetened condensed coconut milk, divided
¾ cup (6 ounces) half-and-half
Ice, for serving

Boil the water. Place the tea bag in a small glass measuring pitcher. Add the boiling water and steep, covered, for 5 minutes. Remove the tea bag and let cool, then chill the tea in the refrigerator, about 15 minutes.

Drizzle 1 tablespoon of condensed milk into a glass. Add a few cubes of ice. Stir 1 tablespoon of condensed milk into the tea in the pitcher. In a separate container, stir together the remaining 1 tablespoon of condensed milk and half-and-half and pour into the pitcher with the tea. Pour over the ice in the glass. Taste. Add additional sweetened condensed milk as desired. Enjoy!

"THE I HATE RACHEL CLUB WAS REALLY THE *I LOVE RACHEL CLUB.*"

Ross

RACHEL'S BLACKOUT LATTE

One night when the power goes out, Rachel finds a stray cat. She heads out, determined to find its owner, and returns with Paulo, a handsome young Italian man, which makes Ross jealous. While Ross couldn't make it out of the friend zone, this swoon-worthy, dairy-optional latte with coconut and hazelnut just might keep you out of it.

DIFFICULTY: Easy
YIELD: 1 serving, 1 cup (8 ounces)
PREP & COOK TIME: 10 minutes, plus 24 hours to chill the coconut cream

¼ to ½ cup Coconut Whipped Cream (page 35)
1 teaspoon granulated sugar (optional)
2 tablespoons chocolate syrup
Double shot espresso
1 tablespoon unsweetened or lightly sweetened cocoa, for dusting
½ cup (4 ounces) Hazelnut Oat Milk (page 31)

In a medium bowl, using a handheld mixer or an immersion blender with a whisk attachment, whisk the coconut cream to soft peaks. If using an immersion blender, use a tall plastic container to whisk the ingredients. Continue to whisk until medium peaks are formed, then continue whisking for few more seconds until stiff peaks form. Check the sweetness, and add the sugar, if desired. Set aside.

Drizzle the chocolate syrup into a mug. Pull the espresso into the chocolate syrup. Dust an even layer of cocoa on top of the espresso.

Froth the hazelnut oat milk for a latte (see instructions of page 11). Heat the milk until the temperature reaches 140°F on an instant-read thermometer. If the milk is not the correct temperature, warm the milk, whisk some more, and swirl and tap the frothing container on the counter to remove any large bubbles. This action creates a finer microfoam. Pour over the espresso. Spoon or pipe the whipped coconut cream on top. For piped coconut whipped cream, use ½ cup in order to fill a piping bag.

PAULO'S AFFOGATO AL CAFFÈ

SEASON 1, EP: 12

"The One With the Dozen Lasagnas"

Rachel's passionate relationship with handsome young Paulo goes from hot to cold when she finds out he hit on Phoebe during a massage. Affogato, a classic Italian treat, is the perfect mix of hot and cold, unlike Rachel and Paulo's relationship. Reminiscent of Rachel's Italian fling, this dessert is an exciting blend of bitter and sweet (coffee and ice cream, respectively).

DIFFICULTY: Easy
YIELD: 1 serving, ½ cup ice cream, plus espresso
PREP & COOK TIME: 10 minutes

2 scoops high-quality vanilla gelato or ice cream
1 shot warm espresso, or 1 ounce extra-strong brewed coffee
Flavored simple syrup or Italian liqueur (amaretto or Frangelico), for drizzling (optional)
Crushed candied nuts from Eddie's Angry Dried Fruit & Sweetened Nuts (page 100), for topping

Place the gelato in a serving bowl or glass mug. Place the bowl or mug on a sheet tray and transfer to the freezer for 5 minutes.

Pull the espresso. Let rest for 1 minute to cool slightly. Remove the gelato from freezer. Drizzle with simple syrup, if using. Pour the espresso over the gelato or serve on the side of the gelato and pour tableside. Top with crushed candied nuts, if using.

TIP: Chocolate-, caramel-, hazelnut-, and coffee-flavored gelato would all be good options as well, although vanilla lets the coffee flavor shine. For a cold version, use cold brew instead of espresso.

"THE FIRST TIME HE SMILED AT ME, THOSE FIRST THREE SECONDS WERE MORE EXCITING THAN THREE WEEKS IN BERMUDA WITH BARRY."
Rachel

PHOEBE'S JINGLE THIEF CAPPUCCINO WITH PEPPERMINT MILK FOAM

This peppermint-flavored cappuccino with a peppermint-candy cookie rim, named after Phoebe's ex-partner, who steals her "stinky cat" song for a cat litter jingle, will make you feel like a kitten lapping up a warm saucer of milk on a cold snowy night. With a drink this sweet, topped with extra treats, it's hard to be bitter, even if your friend and business partner goes behind your back to make a quick buck.

DIFFICULTY: Easy
YIELD: 1 serving, ¾ to 1 cup (6 to 8 ounces)
PREP & COOK TIME: 15 minutes

FOR THE COOKIE RIM:
¼ cup dark chocolate chips (60% cacao)
¼ teaspoon unsalted butter, at room temperature
3 chocolate-mint cookies, crushed
2 peppermint striped hard candies, crushed

FOR THE COCOA PEPPERMINT BASE:
2 tablespoons unsweetened dark cocoa powder
1 tablespoon plus 1½ teaspoons milk
1 tablespoon granulated sugar
⅛ teaspoon peppermint extract

FOR THE PEPPERMINT FOAM:
½ to ¾ cup (4 to 6 ounces) milk or milk alternative
1 tablespoon plus 1½ teaspoons Basic Simple Syrup (page 27) or more, as desired
⅛ teaspoon peppermint extract

FOR THE CAPPUCCINO:
Double shot espresso
Whipped Cream (page 35) (optional)

TO MAKE THE COOKIE RIM: Put the chocolate chips in a small microwave-safe bowl. Microwave on medium for 30 seconds. Stir and then microwave another 30 seconds, until the chocolate is melted, being careful not to overheat. Make sure no water comes in contact with the chocolate or it will seize. Add the butter and stir until creamy. Set aside.

Spread the crushed cookies and candies on a plate and stir until combined. Dip the rim of a mug into the chocolate to coat, then dip the rim into the cookie mixture. Set aside to harden. If needed, place in a refrigerator for 5 minutes to set.

TO MAKE THE COCOA PEPPERMINT BASE: In small microwave-safe bowl or glass measuring pitcher, whisk together the cocoa powder, milk, sugar, and peppermint extract until combined. Set aside.

TO MAKE THE PEPPERMINT FOAM: Froth the milk for a cappuccino (see instructions on page 11). Heat the milk until the temperature reaches 140°F on an instant-read thermometer. If the milk is not the correct temperature, warm the milk, whisk some more, and swirl and tap the frothing container on the counter to remove any large bubbles. This action creates a finer microfoam. Then stir the simple syrup and peppermint extract into the milk. Reheat or froth the milk as needed to maintain the proper texture and temperature before pouring into the base.

TO MAKE THE CAPPUCCINO: Warm the cocoa peppermint base in the microwave for 20 to 30 seconds. Top with the espresso and pour frothed peppermint milk over the shot. Pipe or dollop whipped cream on top, if desired. Serve immediately before cookie rim begins to melt faster than Phoebe's friendship.

RACHEL'S MATCHA SALTED "TEARS" MACCHIATO

Throughout the series, Rachel has gained a reputation as a bit of a crybaby. One such instance occurs when Monica tells Rachel she wants to live with Chandler without Rachel. In this drink, the mix of sweet honey and salty cream cheese balances out the stronger flavor of the brewed matcha green tea base. It's like Rachel's tears, Chandler's cheesy jokes, and Monica's strong personality all rolled into one delicious drink! Sounds like a "matcha" made in heaven!

DIFFICULTY: Medium
YIELD: 1 serving, 1 to 1¼ cups (8 to 10 ounces)
PREP & COOK TIME: 10 minutes

1 teaspoon powdered unsweetened matcha, plus more for garnish
½ to ¾ cup (4 to 6 ounces) hot water (158°F to 175°F)
½ cup Honey Cheese Foam (page 34)
Pinch of flaky sea salt or Himalayan sea salt (optional)

Fill a mug with hot water to heat the mug for a few seconds. Discard the water. Place the matcha powder in the heated mug or a small bowl. Using a bamboo whisk called a Chasen, whisk in the hot water, whisking quickly from side to side until frothy on top and the matcha is dissolved, 1½ to 3 minutes. Alternatively, add the water to an electric frother. Sprinkle in the matcha. Turn on the frother. Froth until completely combined and the matcha is foamy on top, about 2 minutes.

Another method is to heat the water to 170°F. Add the matcha to a mug. Use a mini handheld electric whisk to slowly mix the water into the matcha, adding 1 teaspoon of water at a time and whisking until a paste forms. Continue to add water until frothy.

If using a bowl, transfer the matcha to the heated mug. Pour or spoon the cheese foam on top of the prepared matcha. Sprinkle a small amount of matcha on top of the cheese foam, creating a small circle on top. Sprinkle with the sea salt, if using.

"OH, HERE COME THE WATERWORKS."

Phoebe

ROSS'S DARK & STORMY COCONUT BLENDED COLD BREW

SEASON 3, EP: 25

"The One at the Beach"

On a group trip to the beach, a jealous Rachel convinces Ross's girlfriend, Bonnie, to shave her head. Clearly upset by the turn of events, Ross later says in frustration, "You can see the moonlight bouncing off her head," just like a coconut. Inspired by this moment is a cold brew coffee drink with a hint of chicory, layered over coconut sweetened condensed milk, and topped with coconut cream. No shaved head required to enjoy this one!

DIFFICULTY: Easy
YIELD: 1 serving, 1¾ cup (14 ounces)
PREP & COOK TIME: 12 minutes, plus 6 hours to freeze ice

- 1 cup (8 ounces) Cold Brew (page 26) (use a dark French roast with chicory), divided
- ½ cup Coconut Sweet Cream (page 33) with ⅛ teaspoon coconut extract
- 2 tablespoons chocolate syrup, in a squeeze bottle
- 1 teaspoon sweetened condensed milk (regular or coconut), plus more as needed
- ½ cup high-quality vanilla ice cream

Fill an ice cube tray with ½ cup of cold brew and freeze 6 hours or overnight or until solid.

Make the sweet cream, adding in the coconut extract just before it is fully whipped. Set aside.

Drizzle the chocolate syrup into tall glass. Set aside.

In a blender, blend the condensed milk, cold brew ice, the remaining ½ cup of cold brew, and the ice cream until thick and slushy. Check the sweetness and blend in more condensed milk to taste. Spoon the blended cold brew into the prepared glass.

Tilt the glass and pour the sweet cream over the blended cold brew to float the cream on top. Add a reusable glass straw and enjoy!

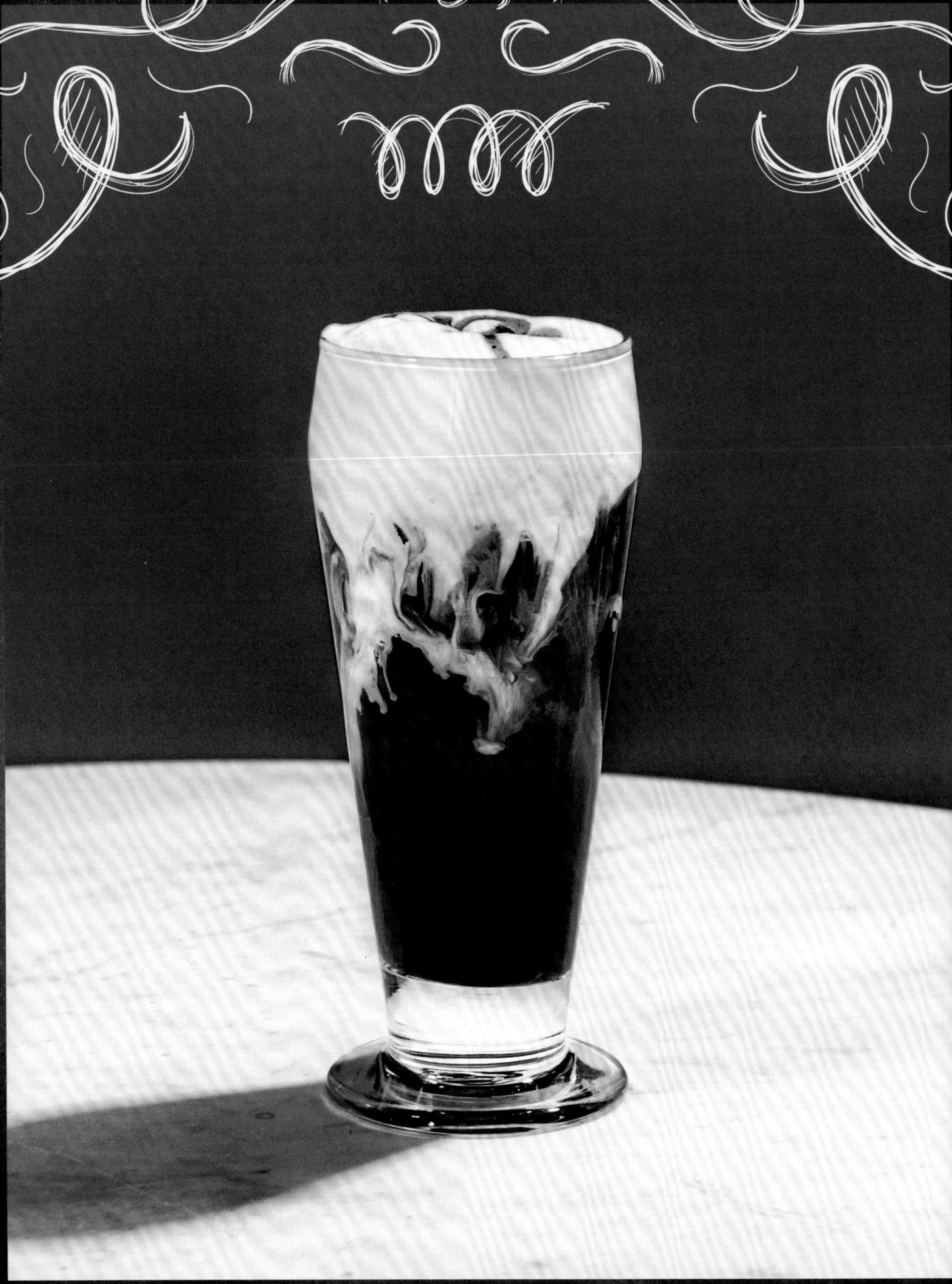

RACHEL'S VANILLA SWEET CREAM COLD BREW

SEASON 7, EP: 20

"The One With Rachel's Big Kiss"

Phoebe once called Rachel "vanilla" because of her safe, risk-free lifestyle, but Ross has a thing for Rachel's warm, sweet side, despite the cold moments in their relationship. This drink is everything we love about Rachel. It's always a fan favorite, unabashedly strong yet smooth with a hint of sweet cream and trendy salted caramel. It's an original, not a copy or a copy girl. It's the real deal and a perfect sip if you need a Rachel fix or if you're just ". . . on a break."

DIFFICULTY: Easy
YIELD: 1 serving, About 1¼ cups (10 ounces)
PREP & COOK TIME: 10 minutes, plus 6 hours to freeze ice

1¼ to 1½ cups (10 to 14 ounces) Cold Brew, divided (page 26)

1 to 2 tablespoons sweetened condensed milk

½ to ¾ cup (4 to 6 ounces) vanilla Basic Sweet Cream, prepared with half-and-half (page 33)

⅛ teaspoon vanilla bean seeds or paste

2 tablespoons Salted Caramel Sauce with espresso powder (page 26), or 2 tablespoons store-bought caramel sauce mixed with 1 teaspoon espresso powder, warm

> **TIP:** Using half-and-half in the sweet cream recipe produces a thicker, creamier sweet cream that will float on top.

Pour ¾ cup of cold brew into ice cube trays and freeze, about 6 hours.

Place the condensed milk in a tall glass. Add the cold brew ice on top and then pour in the remaining cold brew coffee. Taste and, if the coffee flavor is too strong, add some cold water to dilute the cold brew before using.

Place the sweet cream in a small bowl. Stir in the vanilla. Stir and swirl the cream in the container, or use a spoon to check consistency. If needed, with a handheld mixer, or immersion blender with the whisk attachment and a tall container, whisk for a few seconds to aerate. It should be creamy and airy and look like thick melted ice cream.

Tilt the glass with the cold brew to a 45-degree angle and pour the sweet cream over the cold brew. This causes the sweet cream to float on top. For a mixed beverage, pour the sweet cream directly into cold brew without tilting the glass. Drizzle the caramel on top.

> "THAT NIGHT WAS THE
> **ONE WILD THING**
> I HAVE EVER DONE IN MY ENTIRE
> LIFE, AND I AM NOT GOING TO LET
> YOU TAKE THAT AWAY FROM ME."
> Rachel

Morning

{ PERKS }

CHANDLER'S SMOKED GOUDA BREAKFAST SANDWICH

SEASON 1, EP: 3

"The One With the Thumb"

Unlike Chandler's smoking habit, this pretzel bun fried-egg sandwich with pesto, arugula, smoked Gouda cheese, and prosciutto is an addiction you won't want to break. Just don't let Phoebe order you a soda and pass on the tin foil hat!

DIFFICULTY: Easy
YIELD: 1 sandwich
PREP & COOK TIME: 10 minutes

1 pretzel bun
1 tablespoon unsalted butter
2 tablespoons pesto
2 slices smoked Gouda cheese
1 large egg
Salt and freshly ground black pepper
1 slice prosciutto di Parma
About ¼ cup loosely packed
   arugula or mixed greens

Slice the pretzel bun in half horizontally and toast it in the oven until warm and slightly crisp, about 3 minutes. Set aside.

In a medium skillet or nonstick frying pan over medium-low heat, melt the butter.

Spread the pesto on the top inside layer of the bun. Lay the cheese on the bottom half.

Crack the egg into the pan, increase the heat to medium, and cook until the edges are opaque, about 3 minutes. Flip the egg with a spatula and cook until the egg yolk is still runny inside but the egg white is fully set, 1 to 2 minutes (over easy). With a spatula, transfer the egg to the bottom half of the bun on top of the cheese. Season to taste with salt and pepper.

In the same pan over medium heat, add the prosciutto. Cook for 40 seconds per side, or until the edges are crispy and starting to brown. Top the egg with the cooked prosciutto, arugula, and the bun. Serve immediately.

For a cold egg sandwich, let the hot ingredients cool before building the sandwich. The pesto can be added later if packing the sandwich to go.

"WHEN YOU'RE HOLDING IT, YOU FEEL RIGHT.
YOU FEEL COMPLETE."
Chandler

JOEY'S WILD BERRY PANCAKES ON THE FLY

SEASON 4, EP: 17

"The One With Rachel's Crush"

One day, while Joey makes breakfast for his friends, he tries to throw pancakes from the pan to his friends' plates but misses. These souffléed Japanese-style pancakes are fluffy, light, airy, and bursting with fresh lemon flavor. The cooking technique, using meringue in the batter, gives the extra lift needed to go quickly from the plate to your mouth, without missing a beat. Serve with homemade blueberry sauce and your favorite maple syrup. Maybe if Joey had made these airy pancakes, they would have made it to his friends' plates.

DIFFICULTY: Medium
YIELD: 2 to 3 pancakes
PREP & COOK TIME: 35 minutes

FOR THE BLUEBERRY SAUCE:
½ cup fresh blueberries
½ cup water
½ teaspoon lemon zest
1 teaspoon lemon juice
1 tablespoon granulated
   sugar (optional)

FOR THE PANCAKE BATTER:
2 large eggs, separated
¼ cup powdered sugar, plus more
   for garnish
½ cup plus 1 tablespoon cake flour
½ teaspoon vegetable oil
½ teaspoon baking powder
¼ teaspoon salt
½ teaspoon vanilla extract
½ teaspoon lemon zest
¼ cup plus 1 tablespoon buttermilk
Pinch of cream of tartar, or
   ⅛ teaspoon lemon juice

About 2 tablespoons unsalted
   butter
Powdered sugar, for dusting
Maple syrup, for serving

TO MAKE THE BLUEBERRY SAUCE: In a small saucepan over medium heat, combine the blueberries, water, lemon zest, lemon juice, and sugar, if using. Cook and stir until reduced by half and the blueberries burst, about 4 minutes. Remove from the heat. Let cool, then transfer the mixture to an uncovered container and chill in the refrigerator until cool, about 15 minutes. When the sauce is cool, cover the container with plastic wrap or a lid. The sauce can be made 2 days in advance. When ready to use, thin the sauce with a tablespoon or two of water. To serve warm, heat the sauce in a microwave for 20 seconds.

TO MAKE THE PANCAKE BATTER: In a medium bowl, whisk the egg yolks, sugar, flour, oil, baking powder, salt, vanilla, lemon zest, and buttermilk together. Set aside.

In a separate medium bowl, using a hand mixer or stand mixer fitted with a whisk attachment, beat the egg whites on medium-high speed until foamy, about 1 minute (see page 21 for tips on preparing meringue). Add the cream of tartar, then continue beating until stiff peaks form when the beaters are lifted (turn off the mixer first) and the egg whites hold a firm point at the tip, about 3 minutes. The meringue will be smooth and still glossy. If it looks chunky and separated, the whites have been beaten too long. Start over with a clean bowl, whisk, and new egg whites. The meringue can be left in the bowl until ready to use.

Spray a large lidded nonstick pan with high sides with cooking oil. Heat on the stovetop over low heat for 5 to 10 minutes. This method allows the heat to even out and reduce hot spots in the pan.

Whisk ¼ cup of the meringue into the pancake batter. Some streaks and a few white puffs of egg whites should still be visible. Add the pancake batter to the bowl with the meringue, pouring it in to the side of bowl. Whisk by hand using a delicate circular motion, blending the batter into the meringue.

Continued on page 74

Continued from page 73

Circle around the inside of the bowl once, run the whisk through the center, and repeat. This step must be done by hand and not with an electric mixer. Be careful not to overmix the meringue, as it will deflate if overmixed. There should be some white streaks and some small white puffs of meringue visible in the batter. The batter will be thick, light, and airy.

TO COOK THE PANCAKES USING RING MOLDS: Place two or three 1-by-3-inch ring molds in the warm pan to contain the layered batter. Spoon ¼ cup of batter into each mold and carefully smooth out the top. Add a tablespoon of water to the pan, then cover the pan with the lid. Cook for 3 minutes on low heat, then add another ¼ cup of batter to the molds. Raise the heat to medium-low, add another tablespoon of water to the pan, and cover with the lid. Cook for 3 more minutes, then add one more ¼-cup layer of batter to each mold and replace the lid. Cook for another 8 to 10 minutes. While cooking, add a couple tablespoons of water to the pan to create steam. Replace the lid, and cook for a few more minutes, if needed, to set the pancake batter.

When the pancakes are ready to be flipped, the batter should still be springy and jiggly but not fully cooked through. The top will be slightly cooked like pancakes, yet the batter should not be runny. There is a bit of finesse in this step as the pancake batter will leak if it is not cooked enough and the molds are not flipped carefully. Carefully slide a flat spatula underneath each mold and turn the pancakes over to cook the other side. They will not release from the molds when flipping unless undercooked, but use another spatula on top if needed. Add another tablespoon or two of water to the pan, then replace the lid. Cook for 3 to 5 minutes, or until the exterior of the pancake starts to brown and the inside is completely set. Turn up the heat to high, toward the end of the cooking process, and cook 1 more minute to achieve a nice golden brown exterior. To remove the mold when the pancakes are cooked, run a paring knife around the inside edge of the mold to release the pancake. Transfer the pancakes to a plate.

TO COOK THE PANCAKES FREEHAND: Raise the heat to medium-low so that the batter will begin cooking when it hits the pan and not spread out. Using a ¼-cup measuring cup, pour batter into the pan. Repeat to make 1 or 2 more pancakes. Delicately use the back of a spoon to smooth the top and edges of the batter to create even circles. Layer another ¼-cup of batter on top of each circle and carefully smooth out the batter. Repeat the process until you have 3-inch-high pancakes. Follow the directions above for adding water and covering the pan. This method produces flatter pancakes that won't be as uniform, with high straight sides, although they are easier to flip and still taste delicious. Cook for about 7 minutes, or until the exterior of the pancake is a light golden brown and the interior is almost set. Using a spatula, carefully turn the pancakes over and cook for another 6 minutes, or until they are completely set. Turn up the heat to high, toward the end of the cooking process, and cook for another minute to achieve a nice golden brown surface.

Top the pancakes with butter, powdered sugar, blueberry sauce, and maple syrup and serve.

"NO, NO, STAY RIGHT THERE.
GETTING CLOSER."

Joey

CHANDLER & JOEY'S SMART BREAKFAST BITES

Chandler may think he says more dumb things before 9 a.m. than most people say all day, but one smart thing he's done is make these breakfast bites. These easy-to-make grab-and-go breakfast bites can be prepared ahead of time and reheated, freeing up your mornings. Cook a batch ahead in the oven and have breakfast ready to go in a jiffy, or make one portion at a time in the microwave. Pretty smart, right?

DIFFICULTY: Easy
YIELD: 1 bite or 12 bites (depending on prep)
PREP & COOK TIME: 4 minutes or 45 minutes

FOR A SINGLE BITE:

1 large egg, beaten
1 tablespoon shredded cheese,
    such as sharp Cheddar, Gruyère, Comté,
    smoked Gouda, Swiss, or fontina
Salt and ground white or black pepper
1 to 2 tablespoons block-style cream cheese,
    cut into small pieces or chunks

FOR 12 BITES:

12 large eggs, beaten
1½ teaspoons salt
½ teaspoon ground white or black pepper
Pinch of cayenne pepper
¾ cup shredded cheese, such as sharp
    Cheddar, Gruyère, Comté, smoked Gouda,
    Swiss, or fontina, divided
6 tablespoons block-style cream cheese,
    cut into small pieces or chunks

FLAVORING ADD-INS (choose 2 to 3 of the
    ingredients below per egg bite):

4 slices thick bacon, cooked and chopped
¼ cup diced ham or crumbled cooked sausage
Brie cheese, diced
Sautéed mushrooms, diced
Green bell pepper, diced
Zucchini, diced
Fresh chives or tarragon, minced
Baby spinach, chopped

TO MAKE A SINGLE BITE: In a glass pitcher, whisk together the egg, cheese, and salt and pepper. Stir in the cream cheese and any flavoring additions. Pour the mixture into a microwave-safe 4- to 6-ounce ramekin or mug. Microwave on high for 1 minute and 10 to 25 seconds, or until set in the center. The egg will puff up while cooking, yet deflate after cooking. Be careful removing the ramekin as it will be very hot.

TO MAKE 12 BITES: Preheat the oven to 350°F. Grease a standard 12-cup muffin pan or 4- to 6-ounce ramekins with nonstick spray. If using ramekins, place them on a sheet tray.

In a large bowl, whisk together the eggs, salt, pepper, and cayenne. Stir in the grated cheese. Break up and portion out the cream cheese for each egg bite. Next portion out the flavoring ingredients selected for each breakfast bite, dividing them evenly. Prepare 1 to 2 tablespoons of each ingredient or a total of 3 tablespoons of "flavorings" per bite.

Mix up all one flavor combination or make different bites by adding half of the egg mixture to the individual muffin cups or ramekins and then topping with the different flavoring ingredients and the cream cheese. Pour the remaining egg mixture on top of each egg bite before baking.

Bake for 25 to 30 minutes, or until the center of the egg bites are just set.

Remove from the oven and let cool for 5 minutes, then use a spatula or fork to carefully remove the bites from the muffin cups. The bites can be stored in the refrigerator, covered, for up to 3 days, depending on ingredients used. Reheat in the microwave for 30 seconds or warm in the oven for 7 minutes before serving.

MONICA'S LABNEH PANNA COTTA WITH STRAWBERRY HONEY FLOWER

Rachel has soured on Monica talking about giving up her "flower," referring to her virginity. This unusual breakfast option would be the flavor equivalent of Greek yogurt and subtly sweet cream cheese going on a date with an Italian chef and having a baby. Decadent vanilla and creamy kefir labneh panna cotta is Monica's fantasy version of what yogurt should taste like. It's topped with a beautiful strawberry rose "flower" and drizzled with honey. Make in espresso cups the night before, and garnish just before serving.

DIFFICULTY: Medium
YIELD: 2 servings
PREP & COOK TIME: 20 minutes, plus 6 hours to chill

¾ teaspoon gelatin powder
½ cup heavy cream
¼ cup whole milk
1 vanilla bean pod, split and scraped
2 tablespoons granulated sugar,
    plus 1½ teaspoons
Pinch of freshly grated nutmeg
¼ cup light labneh kefir cheese
    (found at specialty markets)
2 strawberries
1 tablespoon honey
Fresh mint leaves, for garnish

Pour 1 tablespoon of cold water into a small bowl. Slowly sprinkle the gelatin over the water, allowing the grains to moisten and be absorbed into the water. Set aside.

In a medium saucepan over medium-high heat, combine the heavy cream, milk, vanilla bean pod and seeds, and 1½ teaspoons of the sugar. Bring to a boil, stirring constantly so that the mixture doesn't burn or boil over. Once the mixture reaches a full boil, remove from the heat and add the nutmeg, remaining 2 tablespoons of sugar, and bloomed gelatin. Whisk in the labneh until thoroughly combined. Pour the mixture through a fine-mesh strainer into a glass pitcher. Pour equal amounts into 2 espresso cups and chill the espresso cups in the refrigerator for a minimum of 6 hours.

When ready to serve, remove the cups from the refrigerator. Carefully carve each strawberry into a flower and place one flower on top of each panna cotta. (Alternatively, slice the strawberries and arrange the slices in a flower pattern on top of each panna cotta.) Drizzle with the honey, and garnish with mint leaves just before serving.

ROSS'S SPACE PRINCESS FANTASY CINNAMON ROLLS

Rachel convinces Ross to share a high school fantasy with her. He confesses he had a crush on a beautiful space princess, with the famous round-bun hairstyle, who was held captive while wearing a "pretty cool" gold bikini. Rachel unfortunately shares the story with Phoebe, who can't resist mocking Ross. She picks up two giant cinnamon rolls, holds them against the sides of her head, and playfully dances to get Ross's and Rachel's attention. These extra-large cinnamon rolls with lemon cream cheese icing are better than mom or grandma can make, and a much less awkward breakfast fantasy. Out of this world delicious!

DIFFICULTY: Hard
YIELD: Three 6-inch cast-iron skillet rolls
PREP & COOK TIME: 2 hours, plus 2½ hours to proof

FOR THE ICING:
3½ tablespoons unsalted butter, at room temperature
¾ cup powdered sugar
Zest of 1 lemon
5 ounces cream cheese, at room temperature
1 tablespoon lemon juice

FOR THE FILLING:
1 cup firmly packed light brown sugar
1 tablespoons plus 1½ teaspoons ground cinnamon
1 tablespoons plus 1½ teaspoons unsalted butter, at room temperature
2 tablespoons cream cheese, at room temperature

FOR THE DOUGH:
¼ cup (2 ounces) warm water (105°F to 115°F)
2¼ teaspoons (1 packet) quick-rise or instant yeast
½ cup (4 ounces) warm milk (105°F to 115°F)
1 large egg, plus 1 egg yolk
1 teaspoon vanilla extract
¼ cup granulated sugar
1 teaspoon kosher salt
2 cups bread flour, plus 1 tablespoon, plus more as needed
1 cup cake flour
½ teaspoon baking powder
⅛ teaspoon freshly grated nutmeg
½ cup unsalted butter, at room temperature

TO MAKE THE ICING: In a medium bowl, using a handheld mixer, beat the butter, powdered sugar, and lemon zest until creamy. Slowly add the cream cheese and continue to beat. Add lemon juice and beat until combined. Set aside. The icing can be made 2 days in advance and stored in an airtight container in the refrigerator. This recipe makes extra icing to serve on top or on the side of the cinnamon rolls.

TO MAKE THE FILLING: In a separate medium bowl, stir together the brown sugar and cinnamon, breaking up any lumps of sugar. In another medium bowl, using a handheld mixer, cream the butter and cream cheese together for a few minutes. Stir the brown sugar mixture into the creamed butter by hand and mix until combined. Set aside.

TO MAKE THE DOUGH: Add the water to the bowl of a stand mixer fitted with the whisk attachment. Sprinkle the yeast on top and stir to combine. Let the yeast sit for 5 to 10 minutes to confirm it's active. The yeast will look foamy on top and clump up. If the water is cloudy and there is no action from the yeast, it is probably dead. Start over with new yeast.

Add the milk, eggs, vanilla, and granulated sugar to the yeast mixture and whisk on medium speed until the mixture is combined, about 3 minutes. In a separate medium bowl, whisk together the salt, 2 cups of bread flour, the cake flour, baking powder, and nutmeg. Add half of the flour mixture to the milk and egg mixture. Switch to the dough hook and

Continued on page 80

Continued from page 79

knead on medium speed until the flour mixture is well incorporated, about 3 minutes. Add the remaining flour mixture, mix for 5 minutes longer, then add the butter a few tablespoons at a time while kneading. Knead for another 20 minutes, stopping every so often to scrape down the sides and bottom of the bowl with a spatula.

If the dough is sticking to the sides and the bottom of the bowl, add the remaining 1 tablespoon of bread flour and continue kneading for another 10 minutes. If the dough hasn't pulled away from the sides of the bowl, raise the speed and knead for another 5 to 10 minutes. Add more bread flour, 1 tablespoon at a time, if needed, to firm up the dough if it's very sticky. In the final stage of kneading, the dough should be tacky to the touch and will cling to the dough hook.

Turn off the mixer and gather the dough with both hands. On a clean work surface, carefully stretch the dough down and underneath itself to create a smooth ball on top. Pat the dough a few times to help shape it. Place the dough in a lightly greased bowl, with enough room for the dough to double in size. Cover the bowl with plastic wrap and mark the size of the dough with a marker or tape on top of the plastic.

Let the dough rest for approximately 1½ hours, or until the dough has doubled in size and doesn't spring back when poked.

INDIVIDUAL SKILLET METHOD: Turn the dough out onto parchment paper or a lightly floured work surface. Roll it out to a 9-by-15-inch rectangle that is ¼ inch thick (or less to account for the dough elasticity). Using your hands, spread the filling on the dough, leaving a ¼-inch strip on the far long edge uncovered. Place the dough on a sheet tray and chill for 15 minutes until firm. Lightly grease three 6-inch skillets with butter. Using a sharp knife, cut twelve 1¼-by-9-inch strips (4 strips per skillet). Roll each strip of dough tightly and secure the strips by tucking and linking the ends under each other. Continue to roll up the strips to create a 6-inch cinnamon roll. Place 1 roll in each skillet or use the no skillet method.

NO SKILLET METHOD: Cut 3 large 21-by-13-inch sheets of foil. Fold the long end of each sheet in 2 inches. Continue to fold, in 2-inch increments, until you have one 21-by-2 inch strip (like a foil belt). Use the strips to create three 6-inch circles. Fold the ends of each circle together to secure the circle or use a metal paper clip on the inside of the foil strips. Place on a sheet tray lined with parchment paper or a silicone baking mat. Add 1 large cinnamon roll into each circle.

Cover the sheet tray or skillets with plastic wrap and let proof in the refrigerator overnight, or for at least 1½ hours, until the dough is puffy and doesn't spring right back when poked.

Remove rolls from the refrigerator. Let them come up to room temperature, about 1 hour before baking.

Preheat the oven to 375°F, then bake for about 20 minutes, or until an instant-read thermometer reads 190°F to 195°F. Wait about 8 to 10 minutes before topping with prepared icing. Serve immediately. Enjoy!

RACHEL'S MIXED "BARRY" CHIA, BUCKWHEAT, AND OAT PUDDING

SEASON 1, EP: 20

"The One With the Evil Orthodontist"

It may not be a surprise to find out that Rachel's ex-fiancé, Barry, hooked up with Mindy, Rachel's maid of honor, after Rachel left him at the altar. It's a little more surprising when Mindy reveals she was with Barry while he was engaged to Rachel. Barry's definitely a mixed bag, sowing his oats while two-timing Mindy with Rachel, and Rachel while engaged to Mindy. Whip up this recipe in the evening, and wake up to delicious oat and berry pudding, and more time for yourself. There's no two-timing here; choose steel-cut or rolled oats—it's your preference. Rolled oats will make a softer, less chewy pudding.

DIFFICULTY: Easy
YIELD: 1 serving
PREP & COOK TIME: 10 minutes, plus overnight to chill

½ cup plus 1 tablespoon oat milk
¼ cup quick-cooking steel-cut oats or old fashioned rolled oats
2 tablespoons cream of buckwheat
1 tablespoon currants, chopped figs, or raisins
1 tablespoon chia seeds
⅛ teaspoon vanilla extract
1 teaspoon maple crystals, maple syrup, or firmly packed light brown sugar
Pinch of ground cinnamon
¼ cup assorted berries

Pour the oat milk into an 8-ounce microwave-safe coffee mug and microwave on medium-high for 1 minute. Stir in the oats, cream of buckwheat, currants, chia seeds, vanilla, maple crystals, and cinnamon. Scrape the bottom of the mug and stir well to incorporate any ingredients that may have settled on the bottom. Cover the top with a saucer and let sit for 5 minutes. Remove the saucer and cover the top with plastic wrap, leaving a small opening to release any heat. Refrigerate overnight. Top the pudding with the berries. Enjoy!

"WHEN BARRY WAS ENGAGED TO YOU, HE AND I KIND OF HAD A LITTLE THING ON THE SIDE."

Mindy

RACHEL'S YETI WAFFLED FRENCH TOAST SANDWICH

Rachel and Monica look for the little round waffle maker in the basement when they are frightened by a scary crazy-eyed "bigfoot," which Rachel calls a yeti. To save herself and Monica, Rachel bombs the yeti with bug spray, but it turns out to be Danny, their new neighbor, who was quite disheveled after spending four months trekking through the Andes mountains. When Rachel later bumps into Danny after he's all cleaned up, she is smitten, but Danny taunts her, suggesting she is shallow and made a snap judgment about him. Rachel tries to turn the tables on Danny, but soon realizes she has met her match. With this toasty, cheesy, sweet, and savory sandwich, don't make any snap judgements before you take a bite. If possible, use a Belgian waffle maker for this recipe.

DIFFICULTY: Easy
YIELD: 1 sandwich or 4 cocktail sandwiches
PREP & COOK TIME: 20 minutes

FOR THE FRENCH TOAST:

¼ cup milk
2 tablespoons heavy cream
   or sour cream
1 large egg
½ teaspoon granulated sugar
1 teaspoon bourbon
Pinch of freshly grated nutmeg
⅛ teaspoon salt
1 teaspoon vegetable oil
2 slices thick-cut (1-inch) white bread
   with a tight crumb, such as
   pain de mie

FOR THE FILLING:

2 teaspoons Dijon mustard
4 thin slices Emmentaler cheese
3 thin slices deli ham
2 thin slices deli turkey

2 tablespoons powdered sugar
¼ cup strawberry or lingonberry jam,
   or other tart jam

TO MAKE THE FRENCH TOAST: In a medium bowl, whisk together the milk, cream, egg, granulated sugar, bourbon, nutmeg, and salt. Transfer the mixture to a rectangular dish large enough to hold a slice of bread.

Using a pastry brush, coat the waffle maker with the oil; be sure to oil the crevices. Blot with a paper towel to remove any excess oil. Turn on the heat to medium.

TO MAKE THE FRENCH TOAST: Coat 1 piece of bread in the milk mixture, letting the excess drain back into the dish. Transfer the bread to the fully heated waffle maker and cook until golden brown, about 4 minutes. Transfer to a plate and repeat with the second piece of bread.

TO MAKE THE FILLING: Spread an even layer of mustard on the inside of each piece of the French toast. Top with 2 pieces of cheese per side. Layer ham and turkey in between the cheese. Close the sandwich and transfer it back to the waffle maker, lining up the grids as best as possible. Close the lid without pushing down too hard—it doesn't have to close all the way. Let the heat of the waffle maker finish cooking the sandwich (like a makeshift panini press) and melt the cheese, about 3 minutes. Remove from the waffle maker.

Before serving, slice the sandwich in half or in quarters and dust with the powdered sugar. Serve with the jam on the side.

TIP: Use a tea ball or a small strainer to dust powdered sugar over the sandwich and plate.

JOEY'S ACHOO BANANA COFFEE CAKE MUFFINS: AKA SNEEZERS

SEASON 6, EP: 13

"The One With Rachel's Sister"

When Joey begins working at Central Perk, Rachel coaches him on how she would deal with unruly customers and offers her waitressing wisdom in three helpful tips. First, the customer is always right. Second, a smile goes a long way, and third, if anybody is ever rude to you give them a "sneeze muffin," also known as "Sneezers." These banana coffee cake muffins have just enough caffeine to keep you alert if you need a second job, like Joey, and are delicious enough to put a big smile on your face. They have an amazing banana aroma that will delight your senses. Don't worry—there's nothing to sneeze about with these muffins!

DIFFICULTY: Medium
YIELD: 12 standard muffins or 6 jumbo muffins
PREP & COOK TIME: 45 minutes

FOR THE CRUMB TOPPING:
2 tablespoons light brown sugar
2 tablespoons granulated sugar
½ teaspoon ground cinnamon
½ teaspoon salt
¼ cup cream cheese
2 tablespoons unsalted butter, melted
¾ cups all-purpose flour

FOR THE GLAZE:
1 teaspoon espresso powder
¼ cup Salted Caramel Sauce
    (page 26), or storebought

FOR THE BATTER:
½ cup unsalted butter, at room
    temperature
¾ cup firmly packed light brown sugar
2 large eggs
1½ medium ripe bananas, mashed
1 teaspoon vanilla extract
2 tablespoons plain Greek yogurt
    (at least 5% fat)
1½ cups plus 1 tablespoon cake flour
1 teaspoon ground cinnamon
¾ teaspoon baking soda
½ teaspoon baking powder
1½ teaspoon salt

Preheat the oven to 425°F.

TO MAKE THE CRUMB TOPPING: In a medium bowl, combine the brown sugar, granulated sugar, cinnamon, salt, cream cheese, butter, and flour and mash together using your fingers. The mixture will look dry with lumps. Set aside.

TO MAKE GLAZE: In a small bowl, stir the espresso powder into the caramel until well combined.

TO MAKE THE BATTER: In the bowl of a stand mixer fitted with the paddle attachment, or in a medium bowl if using a handheld mixer, beat the butter on medium-high speed until extra creamy, about 12 minutes. Add the brown sugar and beat for 5 minutes. Stop the mixer and scrape down the sides of the bowl with a spatula. Add the eggs and mix another 30 seconds. Add the bananas, vanilla, and yogurt and continue to cream the mixture until combined, about 2 minutes.

In a small bowl, whisk together the flour, cinnamon, baking soda, baking powder, and salt. Add half the flour mixture to the batter and blend. Scrape down the sides of the bowl, then add the remaining half of the flour and beat until just incorporated, about 25 seconds.

Line a standard 12-cup muffin pan with paper liners. If using jumbo muffin cups, line each cup with a 6-inch square of parchment paper. Fold and pleat the paper so it fits into the round cup. It's okay if the paper rises up the side of the cup into points. Using a ¼-cup measure, fill each prepared muffin cup half full. Sprinkle 2 teaspoons of the crumb mixture on top of the batter in each muffin

Continued on page 86

Continued from page 85

cup. Top each with more batter until three-quarters full. Increase the amounts of batter and crumb topping for jumbo muffin cups. Top each muffin with the remaining crumb topping.

Reduce the oven to 350°F and bake the muffins until a toothpick inserted into the center comes out clean, 20 to 25 minutes. Transfer the pan to a wire rack and let cool for 10 minutes in the pan before removing. Finish cooling on a wire rack.

Warm the glaze in a microwave-safe bowl on medium heat for 10 to 20 seconds. Place the muffins on a sheet tray. Poke the muffins a few times on top with a ¼-inch-diameter dowel or chopstick. Just before serving, drizzle the muffins with the glaze while filling the holes. The muffins will taste best the day they are baked. If serving the next day, warm for 15 seconds in the microwave and wait to glaze the muffins until just before serving.

CHANDLER'S SCONE, MY SCONE, WITH TART CREAM

One day at Central Perk, Joey, Ross, and Phoebe tease Chandler about his speaking style and vocal inflections. Phoebe explains that Chandler's employees used to like him, but now they don't because he has become "Mr. Bossman." She also reveals they even do an imitation of him. Joey chimes in, mocking how Chandler says, "*My scone*," much to the amusement of Phoebe and Ross, and to the dismay of Chandler. In honor of Chandler, this delicious scone with tart cream will make you the "bossman" of breakfast.

DIFFICULTY: Medium
YIELD: 18 to 20 scones
PREP & COOK TIME: 1 hour 20 minutes

FOR THE TART CREAM:
½ cup heavy cream
2 tablespoons crème fraîche
1 teaspoon lemon juice
⅛ teaspoon salt
1 tablespoon powdered sugar

FOR THE SCONES:
1 cup cold unsalted butter, cut into 4 pieces
4 cups all-purpose flour
¼ cup cake flour
½ cup granulated sugar
2 teaspoons baking powder
½ teaspoon baking soda
¼ teaspoon salt
2 tablespoons plus 2 teaspoons lemon zest
1 teaspoon lemon juice
1 teaspoon lemon extract
1 cup crème fraîche, divided
¼ cup plus 2 tablespoons heavy cream
¾ cup currants (optional)
¼ cup strawberry preserves (optional)

TO MAKE THE TART CREAM: In a medium bowl, using a handheld mixer or a stand mixer fitted with the whisk attachment, whisk the cream on high to medium peaks, about 3 minutes. Add the crème fraîche, lemon juice, and salt. Continue to whisk until the cream thickens and is a little clumpy, about 35 seconds. Whisk in the powdered sugar until combined, about 30 seconds. Transfer the tart cream to an airtight container and store in the refrigerator until ready to use, up to 3 days.

Line a sheet tray with a silicone baking mat or lightly oiled parchment paper.

TO MAKE THE SCONES: Place the butter, all-purpose flour, cake flour, granulated sugar, baking powder, baking soda, and salt in the bowl of a food processor and pulse to combine. Add the lemon zest, lemon juice, and lemon extract and pulse a few times. Add half of the crème fraîche and pulse for 30 seconds. Add the remaining crème fraîche and pulse for another 30 seconds. Add the cream and pulse until the mixture pulls away from the side and balls up.

Transfer the dough to a lightly floured work surface and, using your hands, fold the currants, if using, into the dough. Shape the dough into a loose rectangle. Roll out the dough to a ¼-inch thickness. Fold the dough on top of itself, creating 2 layers of dough, and roll out again to ¼ inch thick. Repeat three times, then roll the dough into a rectangle ½ inch thick. Using a bench scraper or a knife, cut the dough into 18 triangles (or use a 2½-inch round cookie cutter to cut the dough into 18 to 20 circles). Place the scones on the prepared sheet tray and cover with plastic wrap. Refrigerate the scones for at least 20 minutes before baking.

Preheat the oven to 350°F.

Bake until the scones are light golden brown on the bottom and cooked throughout, 20 to 25 minutes. The tops of the scones will be light in color with very little browning on the edges.

Serve room temperature or warm with the tart cream on the side and strawberry preserves, if using.

ROSS'S CINNAMON TOASTY FRUIT TARTS WITH CEREAL MILK ICING

SEASON 4, EP: 6

"The One With the Dirty Girl"

Ross's beautiful new girlfriend, Cheryl, is everything he thinks he is looking for in a woman. Unfortunately, her looks don't make up for her exceptionally untidy apartment. When he first sees her messy apartment, he can't wait to make a swift exit and awkwardly offers her cinnamon fruit toasties cereal at his place. If Ross had offered these cinnamon toasty fruit tarts instead, he might have been able to convince Cheryl to join him at his place. With all the flavors of childhood, these grab-and-go make-ahead apple cinnamon hand pies are everything we love about Ross: sweet and warm!

DIFFICULTY: Medium
YIELD: 8 to 10 tarts
PREP & COOK TIME: 1 hour 30 minutes, plus 1 hour 20 minutes to chill

FOR THE FILLING:
2 tablespoons unsalted butter, plus more as needed
1½ to 2 medium apples, peeled and cut into ⅛-inch cubes (about ¾ cups)
1 teaspoon ground cinnamon
3 tablespoons light brown sugar
1 teaspoon vanilla extract
1 teaspoon cornstarch

FOR THE ICING:
2 tablespoons of Cereal & Cookie Milk made with cinnamon toast cereal and a pinch of ground cinnamon (page 32)
¼ teaspoon vanilla extract
¾ cup to 1 cup powdered sugar, sifted
Pinch of salt

FOR THE TART:
2 cups all-purpose flour, plus more as needed
1 tablespoon wheat flour
1½ sticks cold unsalted butter, diced
2 tablespoons light brown sugar
1 teaspoon kosher salt
3 tablespoons sour cream, plus more as needed
2 tablespoons shortening
½ teaspoon vanilla extract
1 large egg, beaten, for the egg wash
¾ cup coarsely crushed cinnamon cereal, for topping

TO MAKE THE FILLING: In a medium pan over medium heat, sauté the butter and apples. When the apples start to get tender, add the cinnamon, brown sugar, and vanilla. Stir to combine and cook until the apples are light golden brown and tender, about 3 minutes. Stir in the cornstarch. If the mixture is dry, add a small amount of butter. Remove from the heat and set aside.

TO MAKE THE ICING: In a medium bowl, whisk together the cereal milk, vanilla, and powdered sugar to create a thick white glue-like icing. Add the salt. Stir to combine. Add in more powdered sugar and cereal milk as needed to create the appropriate texture.

TO MAKE THE TART: Add the all-purpose flour, wheat flour, butter, brown sugar, and salt to the bowl of a food processor. Pulse until thoroughly combined and the texture is mealy. Add 2 tablespoons of sour cream and pulse a few times. Add 1 more tablespoon of sour cream, the shortening, and vanilla. Pulse until the dough combines and begins to form into a ball. The texture should be smooth, not dry or sticky. The dough should hold its shape when pressed between your fingers. If the dough feels dry, add an additional tablespoon or two of sour cream.

Continued on page 90

Continued from page 89

Transfer the dough to a flat surface covered with parchment paper and a sprinkle of flour. Place another sheet of parchment paper on top of the dough and roll the dough out to a ¼-inch-thick rectangle. Slide the dough and the parchment paper onto a sheet tray. Chill for 1 hour.

Line a sheet tray with parchment paper.

Remove the dough from the refrigerator and let it rest for a few minutes at room temperature (this will make it easier to work with). On a lightly floured work surface, roll the dough out to ⅛ inch thick. Use a 4-inch heart-shaped cookie cutter to cut out 16 to 20 heart shapes. One heart will be a top and one will be a bottom. Gather the scraps and reroll as needed.

Separate the hearts into tops and bottoms. Add 2 tablespoons of filling to all the bottom hearts, leaving a ⅛-inch border uncovered. Use a finger to brush the egg wash on the uncovered border of the pastry dough. Place another heart on top of the filling. The dough needs to be pliable, as to not break the heart. Secure the top heart by crimping the edges together with the tines of a fork. "Dock" the dough by poking the top side with a fork or a toothpick to allow steam to escape while cooking.

Preheat oven to 375°F. Arrange the tarts on the prepared sheet tray and refrigerate until the dough is firm, 15 to 20 minutes.

Bake the tarts until light golden brown and cooked throughout, 30 to 40 minutes. Let cool so they are warm, but not hot, about 10 minutes. Spoon 1 teaspoon of icing onto the top of each heart. Spread the icing as it begins drip, keeping it on the pastry. Immediately sprinkle with the cereal topping, if desired, while the tarts are still warm. Serve warm or room temperature. Hearts can be reheated in the oven, if not iced.

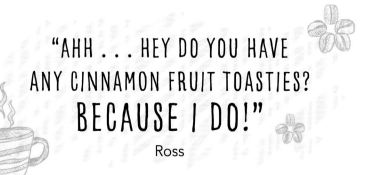

"AHH . . . HEY DO YOU HAVE ANY CINNAMON FRUIT TOASTIES? BECAUSE I DO!"

Ross

MONICA'S PERFECT FLAKY PAIN AU CHOCOLAT

SEASON 6, EP: 18

"The One Where Ross Dates a Student"

When Monica makes pain au chocolat, it has to be perfect. She's a perfectionist and an excellent chef and baker, which has benefited her friends greatly throughout the series. Buttery, flaky pain au chocolat is tough to master, but with some practice, you're sure to have this recipe down pat before too long, just like Monica. Serve with your favorite brew.

DIFFICULTY: Hard
YIELD: 12 pain au chocolat
PREP & COOK TIME: 3 days

Overview:

DAY 1
Make butter block and chill. It can be made a week in advance.
Make the egg wash and the poolish in the evening.

DAY 2
Make room in freezer for sheet trays.
Make the dough, seal in the butter, and begin lamination.

DAY 3
Shape, proof, bake, and enjoy

Day 1

EGG WASH
1 large egg

POOLISH
1 cup bread flour (all-purpose flour
   will work, but bread flour adds more structure)
1 cup water (72°F to 80°F)
Active dry yeast (a little more than a pinch)

BUTTER BLOCK
1¼ cups high-butterfat unsalted butter
   (83% to 85% butterfat)

Day 2 & 3

DOUGH
¼ cup warm milk (100°F to 110°F)
1½ teaspoons active dry yeast
⅓ cup granulated sugar, divided
3¼ cups (462 grams) all-purpose flour with an 11.7%
   protein content, plus more as needed
1 tablespoon buckwheat flour
⅔ to ¾ cup water warm (100°F to 110°F),
   plus more if needed, divided
1 tablespoon salt
12 to 24 chocolate-croissant baking sticks

Continued on page 93

Continued from page 91

Day 1

TO MAKE THE EGG WASH: In a small bowl, beat the egg until frothy. Cover and refrigerate until ready to use.

TO MAKE THE POOLISH: In the evening on day 1, in a medium bowl, combine the flour, water, and yeast. Using your hands, squeeze the flour and yeast between your fingers, and scrape the bottom of the bowl with a spatula to combine. Transfer the dough to a lightly greased container large enough to allow for doubling. Cover with plastic wrap and leave at room temperature for 12 to 18 hours. The poolish will expand and have small cracks on top, indicating it's ready.

Day 2 & 3

TO MAKE THE BUTTER BLOCK: On a piece of parchment paper, use a pencil to draw a rectangle measuring 6½ by 7½ inches, making sure the lines are dark enough to see through the paper. Turn the parchment paper over. Cut and fit pieces of butter and form a rectangle with them in the center of the drawn rectangle. Place a sheet of parchment paper on top of the butter and beat the butter with a rolling pin, working it into the size of the drawn rectangle. A bench scraper is helpful to create sharp edges and helps avoid melting the butter with the heat of your hands.

The butter size relates to the dough size, so measure the sheet tray and silicone baking mat you're using, as that measurement will be the best guide for determining the overall size for the butter block. A 6½-by-7½-inch butter block will fit perfectly with 7½-by-13-by-½-inch dough rectangle once folded inside. The butter block may be stored, wrapped in parchment paper, and placed in a sealed plastic bag in the refrigerator for up to 1 week.

TO MAKE THE DOUGH: On day 2, put the warm milk in the bowl of a stand mixer. Be sure it is the correct temperature. Sprinkle the yeast over the milk, stir, and add 1 teaspoon of sugar. Let proof for 5 minutes. The yeast should look foamy. If not, wait another 5 minutes. If the yeast doesn't foam, it is likely dead and you will need to start again with fresh yeast. Remove the bowl from the stand mixer. Add the all-purpose flour, buckwheat flour, and remaining sugar. Use a spatula to combine and scrape the bottom of the bowl, creating a dry shaggy dough. Return the bowl to the stand mixer fitted with the dough hook.

Remove the cover from the poolish and add ⅓ cup of water to help loosen it from the container. Transfer the poolish to the dough in the stand mixer bowl. Mix on low speed until combined and the dough begins to take shape. Add the salt while kneading. If the dough is not coming together and looks dry, add some more water, 1 tablespoon at a time. Increase the speed to medium-low and continue to mix until the dough is smooth yet still tacky, but not sticky, to the touch. If the dough is sticky, knead in a tablespoon or two of all-purpose flour. Stop the mixer and scrape down the sides of the bowl a couple times during the mixing process.

Transfer the dough to a work surface and knead for several minutes, folding and stretching the dough, from one side to the next and on top of itself to strengthen the structure. Form into a smooth neat ball while tucking the dough underneath. Transfer to a lightly oiled bowl, cover with plastic wrap, and mark the size of the dough with tape or a marker on top of the plastic wrap. Let the dough rise in a draft-free room temperature area for 45 minutes to 1 hour. The dough will be doubled in size when ready.

Punch down the dough to release the air and transfer to a floured work surface. Lift and move the dough with your hands underneath to control shaping while applying medium pressure with your hands or rolling pin. Form the dough into a 7-by-10-inch rectangle, or use a quarter sheet tray as a guide. If the dough is springy, let it rest, covered with a clean kitchen towel, for 5 minutes and then proceed. Line a sheet tray with a silicone baking mat or lightly greased parchment paper. Transfer the dough to the prepared sheet tray and place in the freezer. Chill the dough until hard, about 15 minutes.

Let the dough come up to a pliable temperature. Check dough temperature by placing an instant-read thermometer under it. When it reaches 55°F, proceed to laminating.

TO MAKE THE EGG WASH
In a small bowl, make the egg wash by beating the egg until frothy. Cover and refrigerate until ready to use.

LAMINATING: Roll the dough out to a 7½-by-13-by-½-inch rectangle inches thick or slightly larger. Use a sharp knife to create straight edges after the dough is rolled.

Remove the butter block from the refrigerator and position it in the center of the rectangle, leaving about 3¼ inches open on each side. The exact measurements aren't

Continued on page 94

Continued from page 93

as important as the relationship between the butter block and the size of the dough rectangle. The butter should line up with the top and bottom of the long edge of the dough. The butter should be 7½ inches long, or the same length as the dough. The remaining dough on each side of the butter should equal half the width of the butter, or 3¼ inches.

Fold the dough sides to meet in the center, on top of the butter. Imagine a piece of paper folded in three parts: Parts C, B, A, with B being the butter block and A and C being the dough that will fold over the butter. Pinch the dough closed in the center to seal. The top and bottom edges of the dough will still be unsealed, but the butter will line up with the edge of the dough as it is enrobed.

Roll across the sealed edges to secure and expand the dough to about 7½ by 13 by ½ inches. If the dough is stubborn, let it rest 5 to 10 minutes and proceed, being mindful of the butter temperature. Prick any bubbles that form with a toothpick. Chill the rolled dough until hard, about 15 minutes in a freezer or 30 minutes in the refrigerator.

TURNING THE DOUGH: The dough will be turned 3 times. Keep track of the number of turns and the direction of rolling so that adjustments can be made after each turn.

Let the dough come up to a pliable temperature (55°F). Dust with a small amount of flour and brush off with a pastry brush.

Visualize the dough in three equal sections, like the folds of a letter. Fold the outer third of dough on top of the middle third. Fold the other outer third on top of the first fold, creating a three-layer letter fold with sharp corners and edges. The dough corners and edges should match up for even lamination. Chill for 20 to 30 minutes on a sheet tray covered with plastic wrap in the freezer after each turn (See graphic on opposite page for reference).

TIP: Lamination occurs when the butter is layered between the dough and not absorbed into the dough. The butter needs to be cold yet pliable, about 55°F. If the butter is too warm it will seep into the dough, giving the pain au chocolat a bread-like texture instead of being crisp. The perfect pain au chocolat will shatter when you bite into it.

When the dough is pliable, roll it with medium pressure and make some ripples or indentations in the dough with the rolling pin to expand the dough without overworking it. If the butter ever becomes very soft and seeps through the dough, it means the temperature is not correct and the pressure may be too hard. Cover any exposed butter with flour and immediately stop rolling. Chill the dough in the freezer, on a sheet tray, for another 15 to 20 minutes and start over once the dough is pliable. This step is key to successful lamination. It's all technique and patience.

Repeat 2 more turns, rotating the dough 90 degrees from the previous rolling position after each turn. Chill the dough in the freezer between turns. When all three turns are complete, the dough can be wrapped in parchment paper and plastic wrap and be frozen at this stage for up to 1 week.

TO SHAPE: On day 3, transfer the dough to a work surface and let it come to a pliable temperature (55°F). Divide the dough into twelve 4-by-5-inch pieces. Roll the dough out to 8½ inches long by ¼ inch thick. Roll out a long rectangle, then measure and mark the dough before cutting. Use a sharp knife or pizza wheel to cut out the pain au chocolat.

Place one stick of chocolate on the long end closest to you and roll up with the seam on the bottom. If using 2 pieces of chocolate, roll the dough to cover the first chocolate stick. Secure the dough underneath with a dab of egg wash. Place the second stick of chocolate just at the secured edge of the roll. Continue rolling up the dough ending with the seam on the bottom.

Transfer the shaped dough to a proofing box or unheated oven. Brush the tops with the egg wash, avoiding the laminated layers on the edges. Proof for 2½ to 3 hours at room temperature (71°F to 81°F); no hotter as the butter will melt. Add a container with 1 to 2 cups of boiled water to the proofing box or unheated oven, creating a moist environment. The dough is proofed when the layers are expanded, airy, and jiggle when the pan is shaken. Set a reminder to preheat the oven to 400°F at least 30 minutes before the pain au chocolat are ready to bake. If using the oven to proof, then remove the pain au chocolate and finishing proofing outside the oven.

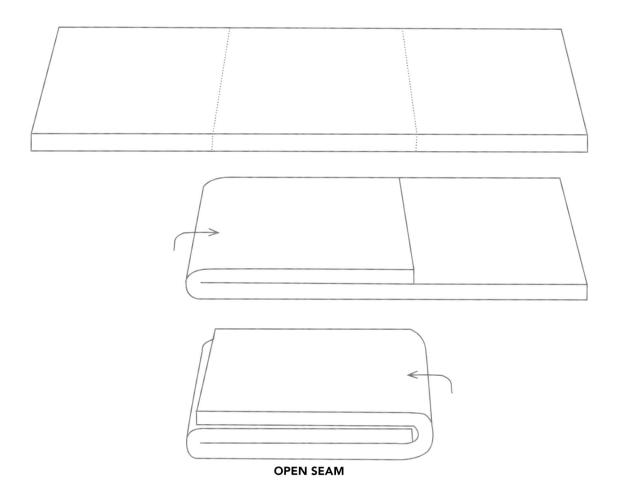

OPEN SEAM

TO BAKE: Bake the pain au chocolat for about 12 minutes. Rotate the tray once during cooking. If the pain au chocolat are browning too fast, lower the oven temperature to 375°F. The pain au chocolat are done when the internal temperature registers 210°F on an instant-read thermometer and the exterior is dark golden brown. These are best served room temperature or warm, after cooling, on the same day they are cooked, although they can be reheated and are still delicious the next day. Wait until they cool and wrap tightly in plastic wrap and store in the refrigerator or freezer. Unwrap, heat, and serve.

"YEAH, I CAN'T SAY 'CROISSANT.' OH MY GOD!"

Phoebe

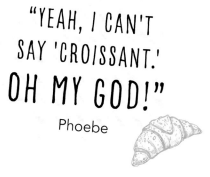

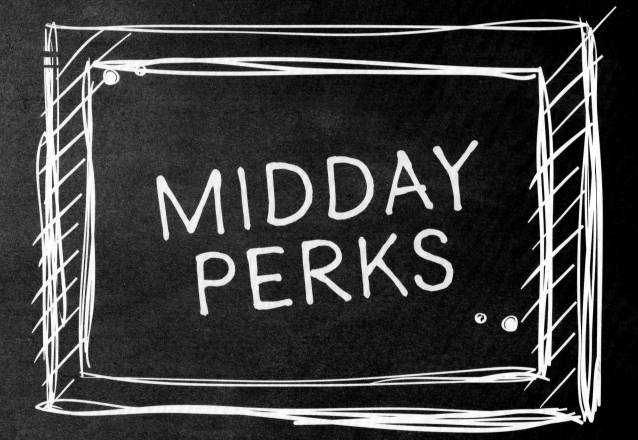

MIDDAY
PERKS

PHOEBE'S RESCUED ROSEMARY CHEDDAR CHRISTMAS TREE CRACKERS

SEASON 3, EP: 10

"The One Where Rachel Quits"

Phoebe is disturbed by Joey's new job working at a Christmas tree lot, because she believes it's not fair for the trees to be cut down in their prime. Joey tries to calm her by saying the trees are fulfilling their Christmas destiny. Things take a turn for the worse when Phoebe realizes the "old" trees are going into a chipper to make room for fresh trees. According to Phoebe, that's ageist and probably not as happy as it sounds. In the end, Phoebe's Christmas miracle comes true when the friends buy up the old trees and decorate them to surprise her. In the holiday spirit of giving, these Cheddar Christmas tree crackers make great gifts and can be paired with Eddie's Angry Dried Fruit & Sweetened Nuts (page 100).

DIFFICULTY: Easy
YIELD: About 6 dozen crackers
PREP & COOK TIME: 1 hour, plus 1 hour to chill

3 ounces extra-sharp Cheddar, finely grated
½ ounce Pecorino Romano, finely grated
2 tablespoons unsalted butter
½ cup all-purpose flour
2 tablespoons cornstarch
⅛ teaspoon cayenne pepper
Pinch of ground white pepper
Pinch of freshly grated nutmeg
¼ teaspoon kosher salt
1 tablespoon cold water, plus more as needed
1 teaspoon minced fresh rosemary leaves, divided
½ teaspoon everything bagel seasoning, divided (optional)

In a food processor, combine the Cheddar, Pecorino Romano, and butter and pulse until thoroughly combined and the cheese balls up. Add the flour, cornstarch, cayenne, white pepper, nutmeg, and salt and pulse until combined. Add the cold water and pulse a few more times. Check the texture of the dough. It should look like coarse meal, and it should be smooth when pressed between two fingers. If the dough is too dry to press together, add another teaspoon of water and pulse a few more times.

Place the dough into a small, resealable plastic bag. Press the sides of the bag to knead the dough. Shape the dough into a loose square, ½ inch thick. Seal the bag while releasing any trapped air. Chill in the refrigerator for at least 1 hour.

Remove the dough from the refrigerator and preheat the oven to 350°F. Roll the dough out between 2 pieces of parchment paper, keeping an even ¹⁄₁₆-inch thickness throughout. Remove the top sheet of parchment paper and sprinkle half of the rosemary and half of the everything bagel seasoning, if using, in an even layer over the rolled-out dough. Fold the dough over itself one or two times and roll out again to ¹⁄₁₆ inch thick. Sprinkle the remaining half of rosemary and everything bagel seasoning over the dough, fold again, and roll out to ¹⁄₁₆ inch thick before cutting.

Use a 1½-by-1-inch tree-shaped cookie cutter to cut out the crackers. Gather the dough scraps and roll out again until all of the dough is cut. You should have about 6 dozen crackers. Place the crackers on a sheet tray lined with a silicone baking mat or parchment paper, leaving a small space between each cracker. Use the tines of a cocktail fork, or a toothpick, to make three small holes in the center of each cracker.

Bake until the edges just begin to turn light golden brown, 8 to 10 minutes. Remove from the oven and quickly transfer the crackers to a cooling rack so they stop cooking. Repeat until all the crackers are made. Let the sheet trays cool in between cooking. The crackers will stay fresh for 3 days in a tightly sealed container stored in a cool dry place.

EDDIE'S ANGRY DRIED FRUIT & SWEETENED NUTS

After Joey moves out of the apartment he shares with Chandler, a guy named Eddie moves in. Chandler quickly feels boxed in as he learns about Eddie's unorthodox habits, such as watching Chandler sleep and obsessively dehydrating fruit. Dehydrating fruit is a fun overnight process, so we understand why Eddie is into it, but he may be taking it a bit too far. Maybe if he'd offered Chandler one of these fruit and nut snacks, things would have worked out better for the roommates.

DIFFICULTY: Medium
YIELD: 18 roll-ups, ¾ cup dried fruit, 2 cups spiced nuts, and 1 cup sesame seed bark
PREP & COOK TIME: 6 to 16 hours (includes a long cook time)

FOR THE BLUEBERRY LEMON DATE (ABOUT 8 ROLL-UPS):

1 pint blueberries
3 tablespoons granulated sugar
Juice and zest of 1 small lemon
2 Medjool dates, seeded and diced
Pinch of salt

FOR THE DRAGON FRUIT LIME DATE (4 TO 5 ROLL-UPS):

One 3.55-ounce packet defrosted frozen unsweetened dragon fruit
Juice and zest of 1 small lemon
2 Medjool dates, seeded and minced
2 tablespoons honey powder or honey
Pinch of salt

FOR THE KIWI LEMON HONEY (4 TO 5 ROLL-UPS):

3 ripe kiwis, peeled and diced
Juice of 1 small lemon
2 tablespoons honey
Pinch of salt

TO MAKE THE FRUIT ROLL-UPS: Preheat the oven to 170°F. Line a sheet tray with a silicone baking mat or parchment paper.

Place the blueberries, sugar, lemon juice, lemon zest, dates, and salt in a food processor, blender, or a medium bowl, if using an immersion blender, and process the ingredients until smooth.

Pour the fruit mixture onto the prepared sheet tray. Smooth out the mixture with an offset spatula, leaving a ¾-inch border around the edge. Bake on the center rack of the oven until the fruit purée is completely set, dry to the touch, and not wet or sticky, 6 to 8 hours, with most fruits taking a full 8 hours to dehydrate. Oven temperature, size, and weather conditions (such as high humidity) can affect the cook time. (If the fruit is dry, crisp, and not pliable, use a pastry brush to add some water to the surface and return the tray to the warm oven until the water is absorbed and the fruit is pliable, 10 to 15 minutes.) Remove from the oven and let cool.

Place a sheet of parchment paper on top of a large cutting board. Peel the fruit off the baking mat and transfer to the clean sheet of parchment paper. Using a sharp knife, and working from one long edge to the other long edge, cut the fruit down the center, creating two halves. Use a knife or clean scissors to trim the edges of the two halves. Roll up each half in a piece of parchment paper, starting from the shorter edge and rolling to the opposite edge, adjusting as needed to make a straight, even roll-up. Use sharp scissors to cut each roll into 4 individual portions and secure each portion with twine. Fruit rolls will last at least 1 week stored in an airtight container in a cool, dry place.

Repeat the process for the dragon fruit lime date and kiwi lemon honey roll-ups. Spread the dragon fruit on one side of the sheet tray and the kiwi on the other side to create a multiflavor roll, or two different-flavored half rolls.

FOR THE DRIED SLICED FRUIT (ABOUT ¾ CUP DRIED FRUIT):

Assorted seeded and sliced fresh ripe fruit, such as apples, pears, plums, and peaches
¼ cup lemon juice

FOR THE SWEET OR SPICED NUTS (2 CUPS):

2 cups shelled, whole, raw, unsalted hazelnuts, almonds, walnuts, pecans, Brazil nuts, or peanuts
1 teaspoon egg white, plus ½ teaspoon if needed
½ cup demerara sugar
Pinch of salt (optional)
1 teaspoon Chai Spice Mix (page 167) or Cajun spice (optional)

FOR THE SESAME SEED BARK (ABOUT 1 CUP):

1 cup sesame seeds
½ teaspoon egg white, plus ¾ teaspoon if needed
⅓ cup honey powder
Pinch of salt
1 teaspoon coconut oil or spray oil

TO MAKE THE DRIED SLICED FRUIT: Preheat the oven to 170°F. Use the convection setting if available. Line a sheet tray with a silicone baking mat or parchment paper.

Trim and slice the fruit to uniformly thin ⅛-inch pieces. In a large bowl, toss the fruit with the lemon juice. Pat dry with a paper towel and arrange the fruit evenly with space between each piece on the prepared sheet tray. Bake for 4 to 6 hours, or until the fruit is completely dry. Turn the fruit at least two times during the drying process. Keep the oven door slightly ajar to allow air to flow if the oven does not have a convection setting.

Remove the fruit from the oven and let air dry on the sheet tray on a wire rack until completely cool, about 8 hours. Dried fruit lasts up to 1 month in an airtight container stored in a cool, dark place.

TO MAKE THE SWEET OR SPICED NUTS: Preheat the oven to 325°F. Lightly grease a sheet tray or line it with parchment paper.

In a medium bowl, combine the nuts with the 1 teaspoon egg white and the sugar. (Start with 1 teaspoon egg white as too much liquid will not set up.) If needed to moisten the sugar, add a few more drops of egg white and stir. Stir together, then add the spice mix, if using. Spread the mixture on the prepared sheet tray. Bake until crisp and light golden brown, 15 to 20 minutes. Smaller nuts and the nuts on the outer edge of the sheet will cook faster. If the nuts are browning too quickly and the mixture is still wet, reduce the heat to 300°F and continue to cook until the sugar is completely dry.

Let cool on the sheet tray for about 10 minutes. Carefully break up any nut crumbles and clusters. The nuts can be stored in an airtight container for up to 2 weeks.

TO MAKE THE SESAME SEED BARK: Preheat the oven to 325°F. Place a rack in the lower third of the oven. Line a sheet tray with a silicone baking mat or parchment paper.

In a medium bowl, combine the sesame seeds, ½ teaspoon of egg white, the honey powder, and salt. Add an additional ¼ teaspoon egg white, or more if needed, to bind the seeds together. On a sheet tray, spread the coconut oil and then the seeds in a ⅛-inch-thick rectangle. Bake on the lower rack until very light golden brown around the edges, but still light overall, about 10 minutes. Let cool on the sheet tray for 15 minutes, then break up into 2-by-2-inch to 3-by-3-inch pieces. Any smaller seed crumbles can be used for smoothies or salads. Transfer to a covered container and store in a cool, dark place for up to 2 weeks.

"MAN ALIVE THIS THING IS FANTASTIC!"

Eddie

JOEY'S MEANIE BOAT SANDWICH

SEASON 7, EP: 3

"The One With Phoebe's Cookies"

When Rachel and Joey embark on an adventure to teach Joey how to sail, Rachel gets a little too critical and hurts Joey's feelings. When she realizes she is acting just like her dad did when he taught her to sail, she feels horrible. The two make up over sandwiches, but then Joey accuses her of wasting perfectly good pastrami. Now he realizes he is acting just like *his* dad. These sandwiches are the perfect meal to share with a friend, whether out on the water learning to sail or at home hanging out. No insults necessary here!

DIFFICULTY: Hard
YIELD: Serves 2 to 4
PREP & COOK TIME: 3 hours 10 minutes, plus overnight for the bread preferment

SESAME BREAD PREFERMENT:
½ cup warm milk (115°F to 120°F)
½ teaspoon active dry yeast
½ teaspoon honey
½ cup bread flour

SESAME BREAD:
½ teaspoon active dry yeast
½ to ¾ cup warm water (115°F to 120°F)
1½ to 2 cups bread flour
1½ teaspoons salt
1 tablespoon egg white
1 tablespoon sesame seeds (not toasted)

FOR THE OLIVE SALAD SPREAD:
6 medium pepperoncini (medium hot), stemmed
2 hot marinated yellow banana peppers, stemmed
1 to 2 jarred roasted red peppers, chopped (¼ cup)
7 large pimento stuffed green Spanish olives, coarsely chopped (⅓ cup)
5 marinated artichoke hearts, coarsely chopped (½ cups)
2 cloves garlic
2 teaspoon sherry or apple cider vinegar
¼ teaspoon salt
¼ teaspoon freshly ground black pepper
⅛ teaspoon ground white pepper

FOR THE SANDWICH:
Olive oil, for brushing
24 thin slices (¼ pound) spicy ham capicola (also called coppa)
24 thin slices (¼ pound) pepper or Genoa salami
4 to 5 thin slices (¼ pound) mortadella
3 to 4 thin slices provolone, cut into small pieces
3 to 4 thin slices Emmentaler cheese

TO MAKE THE SESAME BREAD PREFERMENT: The day before you want to make the bread, pour the warm milk into a medium bowl and sprinkle the active dry yeast on top. Stir in the honey. Let stand for 5 to 10 minutes. The yeast should start to foam on top. If the yeast is not active, start over as the yeast may be old or the milk may have been too hot, which will kill the yeast.

Add the bread flour to the milk mixture and stir until fully combined. Transfer the dough preferment to a lightly oiled container that will allow for doubling. Cover loosely with plastic wrap and place in a warm, draft-free area. Leave the dough preferment at room temperature for 8 hours.

TO MAKE THE SESAME BREAD DOUGH: Sprinkle the yeast over the preferment and start kneading the dough with your fingers. Slowly add the water, then the flour. The dough will look shaggy. Keep working the dough until a ball forms. Add the salt and work into the dough. Turn the dough out to a work surface lightly dusted with flour, or use a stand mixer

Continued on page 104

Continued from page 103

fitted with the dough hook, and knead for a minimum of 10 minutes. Add a small amount of flour or water as needed while kneading. If the dough is hard to work with, let it rest, covered with a kitchen towel, for 5 minutes and then proceed. When the dough is smooth, elastic, and not sticky or tacky, form it into a smooth ball, wrapping the dough underneath.

Transfer to a lightly oiled bowl, that will allow for doubling. Cover with plastic wrap and mark the size of the dough ball with tape or a marker on top of the plastic. Let the dough rise at room temperature in a draft-free area until doubled in size, about 1 hour.

Punch down the dough to release air. Knead for a few minutes. Use your hands and a rolling pin to form and roll the dough into a 7-by-1½-wide disc. Place the dough in a lightly oiled 10½-inch heavy-bottomed or cast-iron skillet. Brush the top of the dough with the egg white and sprinkle with the sesame seeds. Preheat the oven to 400°F. Cover the dough loosely with plastic wrap and a clean kitchen towel and let rise, at room temperature, until doubled, about 35 minutes.

Bake the bread until it's light golden brown and it sounds hollow when tapped on top, about 30 minutes. Cool on a wire rack completely before using. The bread can be made 1 day in advance. Wrap in parchment paper and place in an unsealed paper bag.

TO MAKE THE OLIVE SALAD SPREAD: Mince the pepperoncini, banana peppers, red peppers, olives, artichoke hearts, and garlic and place in a medium bowl. Add the vinegar, salt, black pepper, and white pepper and stir to combine. Cover the bowl tightly with plastic wrap and refrigerate until ready to use. The olive salad can be made up to 3 days in advance.

TO MAKE THE SANDWICH: Preheat the oven to 400°F.

Slice the sesame bread. Place the bread on a sheet tray, cut-side up, and cook until the bread crumb is crisp but not brown, about 3 minutes. Transfer the bread to a cutting board. Use a pastry brush to add a small amount of olive oil on the bottom and top slice. Spread equal amounts of olive salad on the top slice and bottom slice. (For a drier sandwich, reserve ¼ cup of the olive salad and serve on the side.)

On the bottom slice of the bread, layer the meat, starting with 12 slices of ham, the salami, and mortadella, and then the Emmentaler and provolone cheeses. Place the remaining 12 slices of ham on top of the cheese. Wrap the sandwich tightly in plastic wrap. Make room in the refrigerator. Weigh down the sandwich with a heavy skillet on top for 1 hour. The sandwich will last 2 days wrapped. Slice into halves or quarter. Let the sandwich come to room temperature before serving. Serve with additional salad spread, if not added to the sandwich.

"LESSON LEARNED,
RACHEL IS MEAN."
Joey

JOEY'S PASTRAMI ON WHY?

SEASON 6, EP: 4

"The One With the Fake Party"

While pregnant with the triplets, the always vegetarian Phoebe finds herself desperately craving meat. She does her best to avoid giving in to temptation, but Joey steps up to the plate to help assuage her guilt. They strike a deal whereby Joey agrees to go vegetarian for the remainder of Phoebe's pregnancy so that she can eat his portion of meat, leaving the amount of consumed meat unchanged in the universe. In honor of that promise, this delicious sandwich features triple the meat: pastrami, corned beef, and smoked turkey.

DIFFICULTY: Easy
YIELD: 2 sandwiches
PREP & COOK TIME: 25 minutes

FOR THE APPLE SLAW:

¼ cup finely sliced and shredded cabbage
2 tablespoons diced red onion
1 tablespoon diced white onion
1 tablespoon diced peeled carrot
¼ cup cored, sliced julienne green apple
1 tablespoon apple cider vinegar
¼ teaspoon celery salt
2 tablespoons horseradish
1 tablespoon mayonnaise
Pinch of dry mustard powder
⅛ teaspoon salt
⅛ teaspoon ground white pepper
⅛ teaspoon freshly ground black pepper

FOR THE SANDWICH:

4 slices rye bread
6 slices deli-cut pastrami (6 ounces)
6 slices deli-cut corned beef (6 ounces)
6 slices deli-cut smoked turkey breast (4 ounces)
3 tablespoons whole-grain mustard
4 slices baby Swiss cheese
4 small dill pickles, sliced, plus more for serving

Preheat the oven to 325°F.

TO MAKE THE APPLE SLAW: In a medium bowl, combine the cabbage, red onion, white onion, carrot, apple, vinegar, celery salt, horseradish, mayonnaise, mustard powder, salt, white pepper, and black pepper. Cover and place in the refrigerator. The slaw can be made up to 1 day in advance.

TO MAKE THE SANDWICH: Heat the bread on the top rack of the oven until dry but not toasted, about 3 minutes. Set aside. Make individual foil packets for the sandwich meats by placing the pastrami, corned beef, and turkey on a sheet of foil. Sprinkle the meat with water and fold the edges of the foil over the meat to create a sealed packet. Place in a heatproof pan or dish and cook until warmed throughout, about 8 minutes.

Lay out the bread. Spread the mustard on one side of the slices for each sandwich. Lay 2 slices of cheese on the top layer of bread for each sandwich. Top the cheese with ¼ cup of slaw per sandwich. Lay the pickles on the bottom pieces of sandwich bread. Top with the warmed pastrami, corned beef, and turkey. Carefully place the bottom sandwich with the meat on top of the slaw. Flip the sandwich and secure with toothpicks. Slice and serve with a few pickles on the side!

GUNTHER'S MOUSE IN THE HOUSE MAC AND CHEESE BALLS

Phoebe's date, Robert, has a bit of a problem, which has the guys laughing. Ross, Joey, and Chandler share the inside joke, but Phoebe doesn't understand. It turns out that Robert, as Chandler confesses, "isn't as concealed in the shorts area as one may have hoped." Nobody has the guts to let him know, until Gunther blurts out, "Hey buddy, this is a family place, put the mouse back in the house." The secret's out, these mac and cheese balls are incredible, and we suggest sharing, on purpose of course.

DIFFICULTY: Medium
YIELD: Eight 2-inch balls
PREP & COOK TIME: 1½ hours

FOR THE MACARONI:
1½ teaspoons salt
1½ cups no. 35 or no. 41 mini elbow
   macaroni

FOR THE CHEESE SAUCE:
3 tablespoons unsalted butter
3 tablespoons all-purpose flour
1½ cups milk, at room temperature
Pinch of freshly grated nutmeg
2 cloves garlic, minced
1 cup grated Colby cheese (3½
   ounces)
1 cup grated Gruyère or Comté
   cheese (3½ ounces)
¼ cup finely grated Parmesan cheese
1 teaspoon garlic powder

¼ teaspoon ground white pepper
¾ teaspoon kosher salt
¾ to 1½ teaspoons minced jalapeño
   (about ½ a small jalapeño)
¼ cup diced white onion

**FOR THE WHITE CHEESE AND
JALAPEÑO DIPPING SAUCE:**
2 tablespoons milk, plus more as
   needed
¼ teaspoon garlic powder
½ teaspoon minced jalapeño (about
   ¼ small jalapeño)
2 cloves garlic, minced
¼ cup finely grated Parmesan cheese
Salt

FOR THE BREAD COATING:
1½ cups unseasoned panko bread
   crumbs
1 teaspoon garlic powder
1 teaspoon kosher salt
2 large eggs, whisked
⅔ cup finely grated Parmesan cheese

3 to 4 cups high smoke point
   vegetable oil (canola, peanut,
   safflower, or corn)

MAKE THE MACARONI: In a large pot of water with the salt, cook the macaroni per the package instructions. Drain when al dente. Spread the hot pasta evenly on a sheet tray and cover with foil, leaving a small opening for heat to escape. Set aside.

MAKE THE CHEESE SAUCE: In a large saucepan over low heat, melt the butter. Add the flour, raise the heat to medium, and cook while whisking until combined, about 2 minutes. Do not let the butter brown. Slowly whisk in the milk. Continue whisking faster until the sauce thickens and begins to boil. Whisk in the nutmeg and garlic. Transfer half of the sauce mixture to a medium bowl and set aside. Add the Colby, Gruyère, Parmesan, garlic powder, white pepper, salt, jalapeño, and onion to the pot. Return to the stove over medium heat and stir. Continue cooking and stirring until combined and the cheese is completely melted. Add in the macaroni and stir to coat. Check the seasoning and adjust as needed. Remove from the heat and let cool. Chill the macaroni mixture in the pot, on a trivet, or in a separate container for 30 minutes or until cold.

Continued on page 108

Continued from page 107

TO MAKE THE WHITE CHEESE AND JALAPEÑO DIPPING SAUCE: Stir the milk, garlic powder, jalapeño, garlic, Parmesan cheese, and salt to taste into the reserved sauce. Once cool, store covered in the refrigerator until ready to use.

TO MAKE THE BREAD COATING: In a small bowl, stir together the panko, garlic powder, and salt. Set up a breading station with the whisked eggs in one bowl, the Parmesan cheese in another bowl, and the seasoned panko in a third bowl. Use a ¼-cup measure and portion out about eight 2-inch balls of cold macaroni and cheese. Carefully roll each ball in the egg, then the Parmesan, and then the panko, and repeat to create a double coating. Set the coated balls on a sheet tray.

Preheat the oven to 200°F. In a medium saucepan, fill a heavy-bottomed pot two-thirds full with the oil. Heat over medium-high heat until the oil registers 360°F on a deep-fry thermometer (see notes on fry station on page 23). While the oil is heating, line a sheet tray with a few layers of paper towels. Using a slotted spoon, lower a few macaroni and cheese balls into the oil and fry to a nice golden brown color, about 2 minutes. Transfer the balls to a prepared sheet tray. Place the sheet tray with the balls in the oven to heat the center and keep warm.

To serve, warm up the dipping sauce in a microwave or in a saucepan over low heat while stirring. Stir in additional milk or water if needed for a smooth consistency. Check the seasoning and adjust if desired. Serve the macaroni and cheese balls with the dipping sauce on the side.

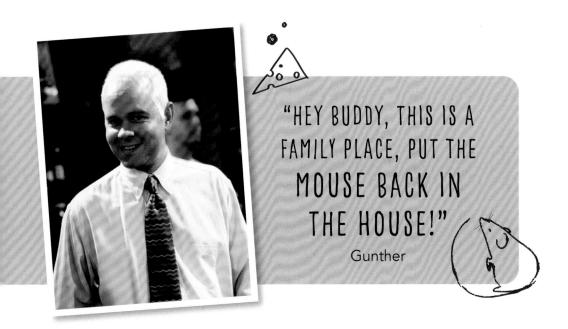

"HEY BUDDY, THIS IS A FAMILY PLACE, PUT THE MOUSE BACK IN THE HOUSE!"

Gunther

MONICA'S DIRTY SUBWAY SALAD SANDWICH

Monica goes on a job interview that gets weird very quickly. The interviewer throws out not-so-subtle hints that her salad making is turning him on. As he proceeds to make inappropriate comments about the produce, Monica bails out on the interview. Perhaps the quick exit and a subway ride home inspired this farm-fresh grab-and-go sandwich. Don't fret, as the recipe calls for *washed* produce.

DIFFICULTY: Easy
YIELD: One 7-inch sub sandwich
PREP & COOK TIME: 15 minutes

FOR THE CREAM CHEESE SPREAD:

¼ cup cream cheese
1 clove garlic, minced
2 tablespoons minced shallot (about 1 shallot)
⅛ teaspoon garlic powder
¼ teaspoon salt
⅛ teaspoon freshly ground black pepper
⅛ teaspoon ground white pepper
Pinch of cayenne pepper
⅛ teaspoon minced fresh rosemary leaves
½ teaspoon everything bagel seasoning

FOR THE SANDWICH:

4-by-7-inch subway sandwich roll, French or sourdough (unsliced)
2 jarred roasted red peppers, drained
1 small dill pickle, or 1 medium chopped pepperoncini
¼ ripe avocado, mashed
10 medium fresh basil leaves
½ cup alfalfa sprouts, rinsed and dried, divided
¼ small red onion, thinly sliced
½ medium cucumber, thinly sliced
2 to 3 white or brown mushrooms, thinly sliced
½ green bell pepper, thinly sliced
1 tablespoon red wine vinegar

Preheat the oven to 325°F.

TO MAKE THE CREAM CHEESE SPREAD: In a medium bowl, combine the cream cheese, garlic, shallot, garlic powder, salt, black pepper, white pepper, cayenne, rosemary, and everything bagel seasoning. Adjust the seasonings to taste. The spread can be made several hours ahead and stored in the refrigerator.

TO MAKE THE SANDWICH: Place the sandwich roll on a sheet tray and warm it in the oven until the outer crust is crisp, 3 to 4 minutes. Let cool to room temperature. Slice the roll vertically down the center and spread an even layer of the cream cheese mixture on both sides. Pat the red peppers and pickle with a paper towel to remove liquid. On one side of the roll, add a layer of mashed avocado, basil, and half of the sprouts in that order. Place a layer of sliced pickles on the other side of bread. Then add the red peppers, onion, cucumber, mushrooms, bell pepper, and remaining sprouts.

Carefully place top slice of bread on top of the bottom slice. Slice horizontally down the center. The sandwich can be wrapped in a layer of parchment paper and foil and refrigerated for up to 1 hour. Just before serving, drizzle the vinegar inside the sandwich.

ROSS'S PRETZELS & "SAY CHEESE"

SEASON 8, EP: 11

"The One With Ross's Step Forward"

Mona and Ross go to Rockefeller Center, but they are creeped out by the pretzel vendor, who takes pictures of her chest. She and Ross hit a snag when she wants to send out a holiday card together, even though they haven't been dating very long. Ross lays on the "cheese," and butters her up while trying to find a way out of the tricky situation.

DIFFICULTY: Hard
YIELD: 6 to 8 pretzels
PREP & COOK TIME: 3 hours

¾ cup warm water (110°F to 115°F), plus more as needed
1 tablespoon plus 1½ teaspoons active dry yeast
Pinch of granulated sugar
2¼ cups bread flour
1 teaspoon buckwheat flour (optional)
½ to 1 cup (50 to 100 grams) cake flour, plus more as needed
2 teaspoons light brown sugar
2 tablespoons unsalted butter, at room temperature
1½ teaspoons kosher salt
¼ cup pilsner beer, flat (no carbonation) and at room temperature
Olive oil, for greasing
Cornmeal, for dusting sheet tray
6 cups water, for baking soda wash
3 tablespoons baking soda
1 large egg, beaten until frothy
4 ounces pretzel salt
6 ounces store-bought spreadable extra-sharp pub-style cheese

In a small bowl or glass pitcher, stir together the warm water, yeast, and granulated sugar. Stir and let rest for 5 to 10 minutes. The yeast should become foamy. If the yeast is not active then it is probably dead. Start over with new yeast.

Remove the bowl of a stand mixer or use a large bowl to whisk together the bread flour, buckwheat flour, if using, and brown sugar. Create a well in the center of the flour. Add the foamy yeast mixture. Use a spatula to slowly mix the yeast mixture into the flour, creating a shaggy dough. Add the butter, kosher salt, and the beer.

Return the bowl to the stand mixer and knead with the dough hook for 5 to 8 minutes on low speed. If kneading by hand, turn the dough out onto a work surface (dust with some bread flour if needed to prevent sticking). Add ½ cup of the cake flour to the dough. Continue to knead until the flour is fully incorporated. If the dough is sticky, add more cake flour, a couple tablespoons at a time, while kneading. If the dough is not pulling together and looks dry, add a tablespoon or two of water and continue to knead for 8 more minutes. Knead until the dough is smooth and clings onto the dough hook.

Transfer the dough to a work surface. Gather the dough into a loose ball. Stretch the dough by pulling on the right side and folding it back over to the center. Repeat the action on the left side and the front and back of the dough. Repeat one more time from the right side. This will strengthen the gluten. Knead about 5 more minutes by hand. Tuck and roll the dough under itself and form it into a smooth ball. While kneading, add a small amount of flour to the work surface only if needed to prevent sticking.

Transfer the dough to a lightly oiled bowl that will allow the dough to expand a couple inches. Cover with plastic wrap and mark the dough size with tape or a marker on the plastic. Transfer the dough to a warm (under 80°F) draft-free area for 15 minutes. Punch down the dough to release air and transfer to a work surface to shape the pretzels.

To shape the pretzels, cut the dough into 6 to 8 even pieces. Shape one pretzel at a time. Transfer the remaining dough pieces to a sheet tray, cover with plastic wrap, and store in the fridge until ready to use. Colder dough will be easier to roll without cracking. Using the palm of your hand, roll a piece of dough into a rope (1 inch wide and 20 inches long). Add a little water to your hands if needed to stop the dough from sliding away.

Taper the edges of the rope and lightly stick one side to the work surface, then create a large U shape with the rope. Grab the two ends and cross one end over the other double twisting them in the center of the U. Bring the ends down and secure them under or on top of the bottom of the U shape, with a 2-inch space in between. The rope should look like a traditional soft pretzel. Transfer the shaped pretzel to a sheet tray lined with parchment paper or a silicone baking mat. Repeat with the remaining pieces of dough until all the pretzels are shaped. Let the shaped dough pieces proof at room temperature, covered lightly with a clean kitchen towel or plastic wrap on top, for 10 to 15 minutes. Chill for 1 hour in the refrigerator, uncovered.

Preheat the oven to 450°F. Line a sheet tray with parchment paper or a silicone baking mat and dust with cornmeal.

In a 10-inch high-sided skillet, heat the water for the baking soda wash. Leave enough room in the pan for the chemical reaction that causes the water to swell up immediately after adding the baking soda (at least 1 inch from the rim).

Add the baking soda when the water boils. It will suds up quickly and take a few seconds to relax. Use a skimmer to submerge one or two pretzels at a time into the soda wash. Use the skimmer to press down the pretzel or a ladle to pour the soda water on top and coat both sides. After 10 to 15 seconds use the skimmer to remove and drain the pretzel. Transfer to the prepared sheet tray.

Score the pretzels on the sides with a razor blade or very sharp knife. Brush each pretzel with the egg wash, then sprinkle with coarse pretzel salt. Turn the oven temperature down to 400°F and bake the pretzels until they are a deep rich brown color, 18 to 25 minutes. Serve with cheese sauce on the side.

ROSS'S DIRTY GIRL GARDEN CRUDITÉS WITH MYSTERY DIPPING SAUCE

SEASON 4, EP: 6

"The One With the Dirty Girl"

Ross can hardly contain his excitement about his beautiful new girlfriend, Cheryl. She's a scientist, works at a museum, and even shares his awkward sense of humor. They seem to have a lot in common until she invites him into her apartment. Her apartment is so dirty that Ross thinks a rat is hiding in a bag of chips. He goes after the moving bag with a toilet brush found on the floor, before learning that it might be her pet hamster, Mitsy. Turns out it *was* a rat! No hunting required for this recipe, just some gathering of farm-fresh ingredients and whipping up a quick Green Goddess Dressing (page 129) dipping sauce.

DIFFICULTY: Medium
YIELD: 2 to 4 servings
PREP & COOK TIME: 30 minutes

2 to 4 baby carrots, with a partial green top, halved

4 asparagus, trimmed

8 snap peas, trimmed, and cleaned

4 radishes, trimmed and quartered

6 cherry or grape tomatoes, whole or halved

2 Persian cucumbers, halved and quartered lengthwise

2 celery stalks, cut into ¼-inch sticks

4 assorted colored mini or regular bell peppers, sliced lengthwise into ¼-inch sticks

6 small jicama sticks, peeled, trimmed, and cut into ¼-inch sticks

6 to 8 mini mozzarella balls, marinated in oil or plain

Sliced artisan bread, for serving

Store-bought marinated cheese, for serving

¼ to ½ cup Green Goddess Dressing (page 129)

Bring a large pot of heavily salted water to a boil over high heat. A high water-to-vegetable ratio will keep the water hot and the vegetables from crowding the pot. Fill a large bowl with ice and water.

Plunge the vegetables into the boiling water. Add the carrots first, 20 seconds later add the asparagus, 10 seconds later add the snap peas. Cook another 5 seconds. Immediately strain the water and plunge the cooked vegetables into the ice bath to stop the cooking process. Blanching makes the vegetables bright and tender. They should still retain a crisp texture. When the vegetables are cool, remove them from the water and pat dry with a kitchen towel or paper towels. Store the prepared vegetables in a covered container or sealed plastic bags in the refrigerator for up to 24 hours.

Arrange the blanched vegetables, along with the radishes, tomatoes, cucumbers, celery, bell peppers, jicama, and mozzarella, in their own sections in a lunch container that has a lid, or place on a platter to share with friends. (Add Eddie's Angry Dried Fruit & Sweetened Nuts (page 100) for a larger gathering) The platter can be arranged 1 day in advance if wrapped well and refrigerated. Add any bread or marinated cheese just before serving. Place the dressing in a small ramekin and serve alongside the crudités as a dipping sauce. Dig in!

JOEY'S ROSEMARY TRUFFLE PARMESAN POTPOURRI CHIPS

Joey's new roommate, Janine, tries to make the apartment a little nicer by adding cute baby pictures, candles, and other "girly things" that Joey just doesn't get. Like the "hot stick" in the bathroom, called a curling iron, and the towels hung on hooks that smell and feel "different." Eventually, Joey decides he can compromise and live with some new things, but we have to laugh when he refers to the "chips" Janine bought as "summer in a bowl." These crisp homemade edible potato chips will fill your home with wonderful aromas of rosemary and truffle.

DIFFICULTY: Medium
YIELD: 1 to 2 servings
PREP & COOK TIME: 40 minutes

4 cups peanut, vegetable, or other high smoke point oil, for frying
1 tablespoon fine pink Himalayan salt, for chips
1½ teaspoons finely chopped fresh rosemary leaves
⅓ cup finely grated Parmesan cheese
2 tablespoons white truffle oil (found at specialty markets)
1 tablespoon table salt
1 large russet potato (about 1 pound)

TIPS FOR USING A MANDOLINE: The goal is to slice the potato paper thin, about ¹⁄₁₆ inch thick. Adjust the blade as needed. Using the guard or the palm of your hand, very carefully slice the potato horizontally. Be mindful of finger placement while cutting or wear a "cut glove" to prevent injury.

Pour the oil into a large, heavy Dutch oven or other heavy-bottomed pot until it is two-thirds full. Heat over medium heat until the oil registers 340°F on a deep-fry thermometer.

While the oil is heating, set up a work area and fry station next to the stove that includes a skimmer, a spider or slotted spoon, and tongs. Line 2 sheet trays with 2 layers each of paper towels. Line a third sheet tray with parchment paper. Arrange the Himalayan salt, rosemary, Parmesan cheese, and truffle oil in individual small dishes next to the parchment paper–lined tray.

Preheat the oven to 300°F.

Pour 2 cups of cold water in a medium-large bowl and the table salt to the water. Use a mandoline on a thin setting to slice the potatoes into ¹⁄₁₆-inch-thick slices. After making several slices, transfer the slices to the bowl of cold water and massage the slices to release the starch. Continue slicing the potato and massaging the slices in the water until only the small end of the potato remains. Discard the end.

Transfer one-third of the potato slices to one of the paper towel–lined sheet trays and pat dry. Replace paper towels as needed and pat dry all the potatoes, removing as much moisture as possible.

To fry the chips, using a deep-fry thermometer, check that the oil temperature has reached 340°F. Place the potato slices on a skimmer and lower them into oil. Slowly stir and dunk the potatoes so they cook evenly, until they look cooked, with little to no color, about 4 minutes. Transfer to the other paper towel–lined sheet tray. Using tongs, arrange the chips in a single layer. If any of the chips are limp and not crisp, place back in the oil for a few seconds and then transfer to the paper towels to drain. Sprinkle the cooked chips with the Himalayan salt. Transfer the chips to the parchment paper–lined sheet tray. Sprinkle with rosemary and cheese, then drizzle with truffle oil. Place the tray in the oven until the chips are crisp and very light golden on the edges, 3 to 4 minutes. As more potatoes are fried, transfer the cooked chips to a bowl, and add the newly fried chips to the sheet tray. Add the toppings to the chips before baking and repeat the process until all the potatoes are fried and cooked.

CAFÉ

Perks

RACHEL'S FIRE GRILLED VEGGIE FLATBREAD

Did you say flatbread or flat iron? In season 6, Phoebe and Rachel's apartment catches on fire, leaving them both without a home. The pair rotate between staying with Joey and Monica. This scrumptious grab-and-go flatbread is inspired by Joey's casual food style and love of pizza, and Monica's elevated gourmet bed-and-breakfast guest-room experience. Add scrambled eggs for Phoebe and Rachel, Italian sausage for Joey, and goat cheese for Monica.

DIFFICULTY: Medium
YIELD: 2 servings
PREP & COOK TIME: 30 minutes

FOR THE FLATBREAD:
2 tablespoons olive oil or good-quality vegetable oil
1 recipe Basic Piadina Flatbread (page 28), or purchased flatbread

FOR THE SMOKED GARLIC BUTTER SAUCE:
2 tablespoons unsalted butter
$\frac{1}{8}$ teaspoon red pepper flakes
$\frac{1}{8}$ teaspoon minced fresh rosemary leaves
$\frac{1}{8}$ teaspoon smoked paprika (hot not sweet)
$\frac{1}{4}$ teaspoon kosher salt
Pinch of freshly ground black pepper
1 clove garlic, minced

FOR THE GRILLED VEGETABLES:
$\frac{1}{2}$ small white or brown onion, sliced into $\frac{1}{4}$-inch-thick slices
$\frac{1}{2}$ zucchini, sliced lengthwise into $\frac{1}{4}$-inch-thick slices
$\frac{1}{2}$ green bell pepper, halved and seeded
$\frac{1}{4}$ red, orange, or yellow bell pepper, seeded
4 to 6 button or cremini mushrooms
6 cherry tomatoes, pierced with a fork, or 1 Roma tomato, sliced into $\frac{1}{4}$-inch-thick slices
2 tablespoons high smoke point vegetable oil
Salt and freshly ground black pepper

FOR ASSEMBLY:
$\frac{1}{3}$ cup grated Parmesan cheese
4 to 6 small mozzarella balls, diced
4 tablespoons ricotta cheese
2 fried or scrambled eggs (optional)
1 small jalapeño, stemmed and sliced in $\frac{1}{8}$-inch-thick rounds
6 fresh basil leaves, chiffonade
2 tablespoons fresh oregano leaves, finely chopped
Hot sauce or sambal (optional)
Salt and freshly ground black pepper

TO MAKE THE FLATBREAD: Rub the oil on the surface of a stovetop grill pan or cast-iron griddle. Heat the grill pan over medium-high heat. Grill the flatbread for a few minutes on each side, or until grill marks are noticeable and the flatbread is warm. Set aside. Leave the grill on for the vegetables.

TO MAKE THE SMOKED GARLIC BUTTER SAUCE: In a small microwave-safe bowl, microwave the butter in 30-second increments until melted. Add the red pepper flakes, rosemary, paprika, salt, pepper, and garlic and stir to combine. Set aside.

TO MAKE THE GRILLED VEGETABLES: Place the onion, zucchini, green bell pepper, red bell pepper, mushrooms, and tomatoes in a medium bowl, drizzle with the oil, and season with salt and pepper. Place the vegetables in the grill pan evenly spaced apart. Work in sections, starting with the onions, zucchini, and peppers, then the mushrooms, flipping when noticeable grill marks are present. Add the tomatoes and heat until slightly charred. Remove the vegetables from the heat once they are cooked on both sides and tender but still firm. Once cool, dice or slice any large vegetables into bite-size pieces. Set aside.

TO ASSEMBLE: Use the back of a spoon or a pastry brush to spread the smoked garlic butter sauce over the flatbreads, dividing it evenly. Sprinkle each flatbread with Parmesan cheese, then layer the grilled vegetables, mozzarella, and ricotta, dividing them evenly. Add the jalapeño.

If you are using the eggs, keep the flatbreads warm on a sheet tray in a 200°F oven while you cook the eggs. For fried eggs, place them on top of the vegetables. For scrambled eggs, spoon them on top of the vegetables, dividing them equally. Top with the basil and oregano. For extra heat, add some hot sauce or sambal, if using. Season with salt and pepper to taste before serving.

ROSITA NACHO TOTS

SEASON 7, EP: 13

"The One Where Rosita Dies"

Everyone knows Joey doesn't share food, and he also doesn't like to share his favorite chair, Rosita, either. When Rachel accidentally breaks Rosita, Chandler thinks he broke it, so he replaces it with an identical chair. Meanwhile, unbeknownst to Chandler, Rachel also buys Joey a new chair. Both Chandler and Rachel are amazed that Rosita seems to have made a miraculous recovery. Joey is jealous of the new chair, with its extra features, that Rachel bought, so he breaks "his" chair, hoping to end up with Rachel's new chair, which doesn't go exactly according to plan. Sometimes Joey is "nacho" smart, but these tots are so delicious, you might break a chair trying to get to them.

DIFFICULTY: Medium
YIELD: 2 to 4 servings
PREP & COOK TIME: 45 minutes, plus 10 minutes to freeze tots

FOR THE PICKLED JALAPEÑOS:

⅛ teaspoon salt
½ cup white vinegar
3 tablespoons water
1 tablespoon plus 1½ teaspoons granulated sugar
1 medium to large jalapeño, sliced into ⅛-inch discs (reserve 2 teaspoons for the bean recipe below)

FOR THE BLACK BEANS:

1 tablespoon mild-flavored vegetable oil
3 tablespoons diced white onion
2 teaspoons seeded and minced jalapeño
One 15-ounce can black beans, drained
1½ teaspoons ground cumin
½ teaspoon chili powder
½ teaspoon garlic powder
½ teaspoon dried minced onion
⅛ teaspoon salt
⅛ teaspoon freshly ground black pepper

FOR THE TATER TOTS:

2 large russet potatoes, peeled
1 tablespoon dried minced onion, or 2 teaspoons onion powder
½ teaspoon garlic powder
½ teaspoon salt
2 teaspoon cornstarch

TO MAKE THE PICKLED JALAPEÑOS: In a small nonreactive container with a lid, stir together the salt, vinegar, water, and sugar. Add the jalapeño. Cover and store in the refrigerator until ready to use. These can be made up to 1 day in advance.

TO MAKE THE BLACK BEANS: In a medium sauté pan over medium heat, warm the oil. Add the onions and jalapeño and cook until tender but not brown. Add the beans, cumin, chili powder, garlic powder, dried onion, salt, and pepper. Stir and smash the beans while cooking. Heat until the bean mixture thickens and the liquid is absorbed, about 5 minutes. Remove from the heat and let cool. The beans can be made up to 1 day in advance; once cooled, store them in a covered container in the refrigerator.

TO MAKE THE TATER TOTS: Preheat the oven to 400°F.

Place the potatoes in a large pot and fill with enough water to cover. Bring to a simmer over high heat and cook for 3 minutes. Drain the potatoes and let cool until they're cool enough to handle. Slice the potatoes into quarters and transfer to a food processor. Pulse until the potatoes are small, like orzo pasta. Be careful not to overprocess or the potatoes will become sticky. Any remaining larger pieces of potato can be removed and trimmed down to size with a knife after processing.

Transfer the mixture to a large bowl and stir in the dried onion, garlic powder, salt, cornstarch, black and white pepper, Cheddar cheese, and jalapeño, if using. Lay a 16-inch-long piece of plastic wrap on a work surface. Transfer half the mixture to the plastic and form the mixture into a long 1-inch-diameter log by carefully rolling up the mixture in the plastic. Twist and secure the ends to keep the mixture from squishing out. Freeze for at least 10 minutes. (Alternatively, place the mixture into a piping bag, with a 1-inch hole at the tip of the bag. Press and squeeze out the potatoes into a long log shape on a cutting board.) Repeat with the other half of the mixture.

Pinch of freshly ground black pepper

Pinch of ground white pepper

¼ cup finely grated sharp Cheddar or Colby cheese

¼ teaspoon finely minced jalapeño (optional)

2 tablespoons mild-flavored vegetable oil, for greasing the sheet tray

1 cup grated Colby-Jack block cheese combination, for topping (pre-grated cheese will not melt as well)

½ cup pico de gallo

6 to 8 slices pickled jalapeños

¼ cup sour cream

½ cup fresh cilantro leaves

Grease a sheet tray with the oil. Using a sharp or serrated knife, slice the log into 1-inch-long tots. Use your hands to help adjust the shape if needed. Set the tater tots on the prepared sheet tray, leaving a bit of space between the tots. Cook until one side is crisp golden brown, about 12 minutes. Use a metal spatula or tongs to delicately unstick and roll the tots to the other side. Continue cooking the other side so they brown evenly, another 12 minutes.

For extra-crispy tots, remove the pan and use a spatula or glass to smash the tots. Return the pan to the oven and cook until golden brown and crispy, about 5 minutes. Keep the oven at 400°F. Place the tots in an oven-safe serving dish or skillet. Top with an even distribution of beans and Colby-Jack cheese. Place the dish in the oven and warm until the cheese melts, about 8 minutes. Remove and garnish with the pico de gallo, pickled jalapeños, sour cream, and cilantro.

"WELL, I GUESS YOU'RE RIGHT. MAYBE I'LL TAKE HER DOWN TO THE INCINERATOR. IT'S GONNA BE SO SAD, AND KINDA COOL."

Joey

CHANDLER'S WENUS REPORT PAPAYA CORN DOGS

At Chandler's job, his boss Big Al wants to promote Chandler to processing supervisor. But Chandler doesn't want the job because he doesn't want to worry about the dreaded Wenus report. While nobody quite knows exactly what the Wenus report is, Chandler won't have to convince you to care about these mini corn dog "wieners" with the New York–style papaya onion sauce on the side. Master the fry game and your cook status will receive an A+ on the dreaded Wenus report; it's a tasty corn dog recipe mash-up. Think Coney Island hot dog meets New York street food. And, surprisingly, there is no actual papaya in the sauce. It's another Wenus report mystery.

DIFFICULTY: Medium
YIELD: 10 to 12 mini corn dogs
PREP & COOK TIME: 1½ hours

FOR THE PAPAYA ONION SAUCE:
1½ tablespoon unsalted butter
1 medium white or brown onion, thinly sliced
¾ teaspoon salt
1 medium yellow bell pepper, thinly sliced
½ teaspoon red pepper flakes
1 clove garlic, minced
⅛ teaspoon ground cinnamon
½ teaspoon chili powder
⅛ teaspoon ground white pepper, plus more to taste
2 tablespoons ketchup
1 teaspoon light brown sugar
1 tablespoon white or apple cider vinegar, plus more to taste

FOR THE CORN DOG BATTER:
½ cup fine yellow cornmeal (or pulse medium cornmeal in food processor until fine)
½ cup plus 1 tablespoon all-purpose flour, plus more to thicken batter if needed
1 tablespoon plus 1½ teaspoons granulated sugar, or 2 tablespoons honey powder
¼ teaspoon mustard powder
½ teaspoon onion powder
2 tablespoons baking powder
½ teaspoon salt
Pinch of cayenne pepper, optional
1 large egg, whisked
½ cup buttermilk, plus slightly more to loosen batter if needed
Pinch of cayenne pepper (optional)

FOR THE CORN DOGS:
High smoke point vegetable oil, for frying
¼ cup cornstarch, for dusting the hot dogs
4 all-beef franks, cut into thirds, plus more for testing the oil
15 candy apple sticks, or 4½-inch-long wooden skewers for corn, plus more for testing
Store-bought dark whole-grain mustard, for serving (optional)

TIPS: Make the sauce and batter ahead of time. Cut and skewer the hot dogs the night before and refrigerate them, wrapped, until ready to use.

TO MAKE THE PAPAYA ONION SAUCE: In a medium sauté pan over medium-low heat, combine the butter, onion, salt, and 2 tablespoons of water and sweat the onion. Don't allow the onions to brown. When the onions are tender, add the yellow pepper, red pepper flakes, and garlic. Cook for 20 minutes, stirring as needed. Add small amounts of water throughout the cooking process to keep the sauce from evaporating.

Add the cinnamon, chili powder, and white pepper, and cook another 10 minutes. Add the ketchup, brown sugar, and vinegar. Stir in about ¼ cup of water and cook another 10 to 15 minutes. The liquid should have a thick-sauce consistency, like ketchup. Remove from the heat. Let cool to a slightly warm stage, then transfer to a blender. Blend until smooth, about 4 minutes. Check the seasoning and adjust as needed, adding salt, pepper, or a little vinegar to taste. The sauce may be made up to 5 days in advance and stored in an airtight container in the refrigerator. Warm the sauce in a saucepan, or heat in a microwave, before serving.

Continued on page 122

Continued from page 121

TO MAKE THE CORN DOG BATTER: In a medium bowl, whisk together the cornmeal, flour, granulated sugar, mustard powder, onion powder, baking powder, salt, and cayenne, if using. In a separate medium bowl, stir together the egg and buttermilk.

Add the egg mixture to the cornmeal mixture and whisk thoroughly to combine. The mixture should resemble very thick pancake batter. Pour the batter into a tall narrow container or drinking glass to make dipping the corn dogs easier. The batter can be made several hours before cooking and stored in the refrigerator until ready to use. Let the batter and hot dogs come to room temperature for 15 minutes before frying. The batter may thicken up; stir in a little buttermilk, if needed, to thin it. If the batter seems too thin, stir in another tablespoon of flour.

TO MAKE THE CORN DOGS: Fill a medium, deep pot with at least 5 inches of oil (see notes on fry station on page 23). The pot should have sufficient room for the oil to rise at least 2 inches while frying. Heat the oil over medium-high heat to between 360°F and 375°F (use a candy or deep-fry thermometer to check the temp).

Line a sheet tray with two layers of paper towels and set it near the stovetop. While the oil is heating, spread the cornstarch across a flat dish. To coat the hot dogs with batter, dry the hot dog skins with paper towels, then roll them in the cornstarch until evenly coated. Insert a skewer into the end of each hot dog, about ¾ inch deep. Holding a hot dog by its skewer, dip the hot dog into the batter deep enough to cover ¼ inch of the skewer, wiggle the hot dog in the batter, lift the hot dog out of the batter, and repeat two more times to ensure a proper coating. On the last coating, twist the hot dog up while lifting it out of batter. Gently flick your wrist while lifting up the hot dog, and roll any excess batter back on top of the tip of the hot dog creating a little point. Place the coated hot dog immediately into the oil and repeat with the remaining hot dogs, frying each hot dog immediately after dipping.

Don't add more than 3 corn dogs to the oil at a time. Slowly submerge the corn dogs in the hot oil and let go. Use tongs to rotate the corn dogs so that they cook evenly. Cook for 3 to 4 minutes, using tongs or a skimmer to keep the corn dogs submerged in the oil while cooking. Cut through the first corn dog to test for doneness and confirm cook time and texture. The batter should be cooked throughout, and light golden brown on the exterior. The hot dog internal temperature should be at least 165°F on an instant-read thermometer. Adjust the cook time and heat as needed. Maintain the oil temperature between 360°F to 375°F. Use a wire skimmer to remove any burned bits of batter. Double fry the corn dogs. Add them back into the oil and cook another 2 minutes until deep golden brown. The second fry will create a crisp exterior texture and fluffy fully cooked batter interior, while preventing the batter from over browning with a one fry method.

Transfer the cooked corn dogs to the paper towel–lined sheet tray, rolling them gently to blot excess oil. The cooked corn dog batter should be crisp, firm, and golden brown.

Serve immediately with famous papaya onion sauce or mustard and a glass of chilled papaya juice.

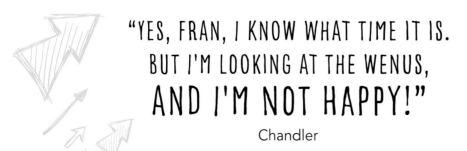

"YES, FRAN, I KNOW WHAT TIME IT IS.
BUT I'M LOOKING AT THE WENUS,
AND I'M NOT HAPPY!"
Chandler

ROSS'S BLACKENED TURKEY MELT WITH CAJUN AIOLI

When the friends are locked out of the apartment one Thanksgiving because Rachel thought Monica had the keys and Monica thought she had asked Rachel to get the keys, the turkey Monica was cooking burns and the meal is ruined. This blackened Cajun turkey melt is a nod to the burned bird, and to how the friends always end up making Thanksgiving moments to savor in spite of any missteps. This zesty turkey underdog is so good Ross just might swap his traditional "moist maker" sandwich for it.

DIFFICULTY: Easy
YIELD: 1 sandwich
PREP & COOK TIME: 13 minutes

FOR THE CAJUN AIOLI:
¼ cup mayonnaise
1 teaspoon relish
2 tablespoons ketchup
2 teaspoons Cajun spice blend
Pinch of salt
Pinch of ground white pepper
1 clove garlic, minced

FOR THE SANDWICH:
2 pieces roast turkey, cut ¼ inch thick (not deli meat)
¼ cup sauerkraut, drained and 1½ tablespoons juice reserved
Pinch of Cajun spice blend
2 slices rye bread
3 slices Swiss cheese (about 2 ounces)

Preheat the oven to 350°F.

TO MAKE THE CAJUN AIOLI: In a medium bowl, combine the mayonnaise, relish, ketchup, Cajun spice blend, salt, white pepper, and garlic until creamy. The aioli can be made 1 day in advance and stored in a tightly covered container in the refrigerator.

TO MAKE THE SANDWICH: Make a foil packet for the sliced turkey. Place the turkey on a piece of aluminum foil and drizzle sauerkraut juice on top. Sprinkle a pinch of Cajun spice blend on the turkey and seal the packet by folding the foil over the turkey. Place the packet in a heatproof pan in the oven for 8 minutes to steam.

Meanwhile, warm the bread in the oven directly on the rack, until crisp but not toasted, about 5 minutes.

Lightly oil a cast-iron skillet or nonstick pan. Remove the bread and turkey from the oven. Spread a thin layer of aioli on the outer side of each bread slice. Place the bread, aioli-side down, in the skillet. Layer each piece of bread with cheese to cover. Remove the turkey from the foil and drain. Place on top of the cheese. Top with sauerkraut. Place the skillet over medium heat and cook the bread until slightly brown. Carefully flip one slice on top of the other and weigh down the sandwich with a heavy skillet. Continue cooking until the bread is golden brown and crisp. Using a spatula, transfer the sandwich to a plate. Carefully open the sandwich and add a layer of aioli in the center. Close the sandwich, slice, and serve with more aioli on the side.

JOEY'S "DON'T BE JELLY!" FISH PIADINA SANDWICH

On a trip the group takes to the beach, Monica is stung by a jellyfish. Joey remembers seeing a less-than-desirable way to stop the pain on a TV show. They return to the beach house so overcome with shame they can't even look at each other. When Rachel asks what happened out there, Monica, Chandler, and Joey won't confess, because they made a secret pact to never speak of the event again. This delicious fish sandwich is a much more pleasant beach memory the group wishes they shared instead!

DIFFICULTY: Medium
YIELD: 1 sandwich
PREP & COOK TIME: 35 minutes, plus 4 hours to chill the dough

FOR THE DILL SAUCE:
½ cup sour cream
1 to 2 cloves garlic, minced
2 tablespoons minced shallot,
    (about 1 small shallot)
Juice of 1 small lemon
1 tablespoon mayonnaise
¼ teaspoon Dijon mustard
¼ teaspoon salt
⅛ teaspoon ground white pepper
Freshly ground black pepper
3 tablespoons finely chopped fresh dill
    (2 to 3 sprigs)

FOR THE ROASTED CHERRY TOMATO SPREAD:
1 cup cherry tomatoes (about 20 tomatoes)
1 tablespoon vegetable oil
Salt and freshly ground black pepper

FOR THE SALMON:
Vegetable oil, for coating
Two 4-ounce pieces salmon with skin
    (wild caught preferred)
½ teaspoon kosher salt
⅛ teaspoon ground white pepper
⅛ teaspoon freshly ground black pepper

FOR THE SANDWICH:
1 Basic Piadina Flatbread (page 28)
1 cup baby arugula
1 lemon, cut into wedges and seeded
¼ teaspoon salt
⅛ teaspoon freshly ground black pepper

TO MAKE THE DILL SAUCE: In a medium bowl, combine the sour cream, garlic, shallot, lemon juice, mayonnaise, mustard, salt, white pepper, and black pepper. Cover and refrigerate for 4 hours or overnight. Reserve the fresh dill to add later.

TO MAKE THE ROASTED CHERRY TOMATO SPREAD: Preheat the oven to 400°F.

Place the tomatoes in an ovenproof dish or skillet. Drizzle with the oil, sprinkle with salt and pepper, and pierce each tomato with a sharp knife. Roast until the tomato skins blister and start to burn, about 20 minutes. Transfer the tomatoes to a bowl, then smash and stir the tomatoes to create a chunky paste. Let cool and refrigerate, covered, until ready to use. The spread can be made 1 day in advance.

TO MAKE THE SALMON: Spray a heavy skillet or stovetop grill with a light coating of vegetable oil and heat over high heat. While the pan is heating, dry the salmon thoroughly with paper towels. Rub the salmon with a small amount of oil and equally season each side with the salt, white pepper, and black pepper.

Reduce the heat to medium-high. Place the salmon, skin-side down, in the pan and cook for about 4 minutes, until the flesh is a creamy salmon color and firm, and the skin is crisp. Flip the fish and cook the other side, 2 to 3 minutes. Transfer the salmon to a plate to cool.

TO MAKE THE SANDWICH: Spread the cherry tomato spread on the inside of the flatbread. Place the arugula in a small bowl, squeeze the lemon over it, and add the salt and pepper. Place the arugula on half of the flatbread. Cut the salmon into bite-size pieces, saving the crispy skin to include in the sandwich, if desired. Add the salmon, salmon skin, and then dill sauce and reserved fresh dill. Fold over the flatbread and serve immediately.

MR. TREEGER'S SUPER-TRASHY NEW YORK PIZZA ROLLS

When Rachel goes to the trash chute to throw away her empty pizza box, Mr. Treeger gives her a hard time for not breaking it down first. Rachel tries to roll with it, acting like she doesn't know what Treeger is talking about, but he persists, eventually making her cry as she leaves with the pizza box. Joey confronts Mr. Treeger, and in a strange turn of events, ends up practicing ballroom dancing with him. Sometimes you have to just (pizza) roll with it.

DIFFICULTY: Medium
YIELD: 7 to 8 pizza rolls
PREP & COOK TIME: 1 hour

FOR THE GARLIC BUTTER DIPPING SAUCE:
4 tablespoons unsalted butter
½ teaspoon salt
2 cloves garlic, minced

FOR THE FILLING:
1 tablespoon plus 1½ teaspoons unsalted butter
1 cup button or cremini mushrooms, cut into small dice
2 cloves garlic, minced
⅛ teaspoon red pepper flakes
¼ teaspoon salt
½ cup small diced white onion
¾ cup small diced green bell pepper
¼ cup small diced red, orange, or yellow bell pepper
½ cup cubed pepperoni
¼ cup prepared unsweetened marinara sauce
1 tablespoon finely chopped fresh oregano leaves
¼ teaspoon smoked Spanish paprika
¼ teaspoon garlic powder
¼ teaspoon freshly ground black pepper
¼ teaspoon ground white pepper
4 ounces water-packed mozzarella, cut into small dice
¾ cup finely grated Parmesan Cheese
1 large egg, beaten
Fresh egg roll wrappers, for rolling
3 to 4 cups vegetable oil

TO MAKE THE GARLIC BUTTER DIPPING SAUCE: In a small microwave-safe bowl, melt the butter in the microwave on medium heat in 30-second increments. Add the salt and garlic and stir to combine. Set aside.

TO MAKE THE FILLING: In a medium sauté pan or cast-iron skillet over medium heat, melt the butter. Add the mushrooms and cook until they begin to release their liquid. Add the garlic, red pepper flakes, and salt and stir to combine. Add the onion and cook for 1 minute. Add the green and red bell peppers and pepperoni. Cook for 1 minute, until the peppers are lightly tender. Remove from the heat.

In a medium bowl, stir together the marinara sauce, oregano, paprika, garlic powder, black pepper, white pepper, and salt.

Add the marinara mixture, mozzarella, and Parmesan cheese to the mushroom mixture. Let the mixture cool before filling the wrappers.

To wrap the pizza rolls, set up a workstation with the beaten egg, the mushroom pepperoni filling, a ¼-cup measuring cup, and the egg roll wrappers. On a work surface, lay out one egg roll wrapper with a corner at the top and bottom like a diamond shape. Place ¼ cup of the filling in a 1½-inch rectangle toward the middle of the diamond shape. Brush the beaten egg on the bottom three corners of the wrapper with a pastry brush. Bring the bottom corner of the diamond up and over the filling. Then tuck the tip of the wrapper just

Continued on page 128

Continued from page 127

under the filling. Fold in the two sides of the wrapper, over the center filling, and push the filling in to tighten up the roll in the center and remove any air pockets. Continue to roll the wrapper to the farthest tip of the diamond shape, using your fingers to guide the roll, and keep the filling in place as you roll it up. Add additional beaten egg to the top tip and roll the wrapper up into a small burrito shape. Continue until all pizza rolls are wrapped.

Preheat the oven to 300°F.

Fill a large, heavy-bottomed pot two-thirds full with oil and heat over medium heat until the oil registers 370°F on a deep-fry thermometer (see notes on fry station on page 23). Line a sheet tray with several layers of paper towels.

Using a spider or a slotted spoon, lower 1 or 2 pizza rolls into the oil at a time. Fry for about 2 minutes per side, turning the rolls as they begin to brown. Check the oil temperature frequently and adjust the heat as needed to maintain a temperature of between 360°F to 370°F. The pizza rolls should be golden brown and will continue to cook once removed from the oil. Be careful not to overcook or undercook. Test a roll and confirm cooking time. The rolls should be golden brown on the outside with the wrapper fully cooked inside (no raw dough) and the filling temperature should register above 165°F on an instant-read thermometer. Transfer the cooked pizza rolls from the oil to the prepared sheet tray to drain. Place the cooked and drained rolls on a sheet tray and place in the oven to keep the pizza rolls warm. Place the garlic butter in a ramekin and warm in the microwave for 30 seconds. Serve alongside the hot pizza rolls. Serve pizza rolls whole or sliced on the diagonal through the center of each roll.

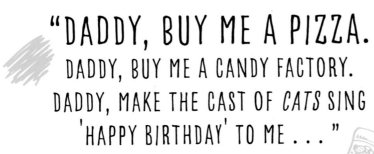

"DADDY, BUY ME A PIZZA.
DADDY, BUY ME A CANDY FACTORY.
DADDY, MAKE THE CAST OF *CATS* SING 'HAPPY BIRTHDAY' TO ME . . . "

Mr. Treeger

RACHEL'S GRILLED SHRIMP COBB SALAD WRAPS FOR TWO—EXTRA TIP

Rachel's dad is known for being cheap when it comes to tipping waitstaff, leaving only a 4 percent tip on their fancy lobster meal. Feeling guilty, Ross leaves an extra $20 tip, which Mr. Green finds offensive. If Mr. Green had ordered these shrimp Cobb salad wraps instead of lobster, he would have had some more money left over for the tip and might have avoided the contentious encounter with Ross.

DIFFICULTY: Medium
YIELD: 2 servings
PREP & COOK TIME: 40 minutes

FOR THE GREEN GODDESS DRESSING:
1 teaspoon capers, or ⅛ teaspoon anchovy
2 tablespoons chopped fresh chives
1 green onion, chopped
¼ cup loosely packed chopped parsley
2 tablespoons chopped fresh tarragon leaves
¼ cup mayonnaise
¼ cup sour cream
1½ tablespoons lemon juice
⅛ teaspoon salt
Ground white pepper
Freshly ground black pepper

FOR THE GRILLED SHRIMP:
2 cloves garlic, minced
1 tablespoon chopped fresh chives
1 tablespoon chopped fresh parsley
2 tablespoons vegetable oil, plus more for the grill
½ teaspoon salt
Pinch of ground white pepper
Pinch of freshly ground black pepper
18 to 20 medium shrimp, thawed, peeled, and deveined
1 lemon, cut into wedges

4 Basic Piadina Flatbread (page 28) or tortillas (optional)
8 sturdy lettuce leaves, such as romaine, iceberg, green leaf, or butter lettuce, rinsed and dried
2 thick-cut bacon slices, cooked and chopped
1 hard-boiled egg, thinly sliced
1 small avocado, diced
¼ cup crumbled Roquefort cheese
2 tablespoons diced green onion
12 cherry tomatoes, quartered

TIP: For perfect hard-boiled eggs, add water into a large pot. Insert a steamer basket and bring the water to a boil. Add the eggs and cook for 12 to 15 minutes. Remove the eggs and drop into cold water. Immediately roll the eggs back and forth to remove shell.

Continued on page 131

Continued from page 129

TO MAKE THE GREEN GODDESS DRESSING: Combine the capers, chives, onion, parsley, tarragon, mayonnaise, sour cream, lemon juice, and salt in a food processor. Season with white and black pepper and pulse until creamy. This dressing is best the day it is made, but it will last for 2 days stored in a tightly covered container in the refrigerator. Stir before using.

TO MAKE THE GRILLED SHRIMP: In a medium bowl, stir together the garlic, chives, parsley, oil, salt, and white and black pepper. Add the shrimp. Marinate the shrimp for 10 minutes in the refrigerator. Prep the grill with some oil to prevent sticking and heat to medium-high. Transfer the shrimp to the grill and cook about 3 minutes per side, until the shrimp are opaque inside and cooked through. Transfer the shrimp to a platter. Squeeze the lemon over the shrimp and adjust the seasoning as needed. Chop the shrimp into ¼-inch cubes and place in a bowl. Chill.

To serve, heat or grill the flatbreads, if using, over medium-high heat for about 2 minutes per side. Divide the lettuce evenly between two bowls. Divide the bacon, egg, avocado, cheese, onion, tomatoes, and grilled shrimp equally between the two bowls. Drizzle with dressing. Use the flatbreads or tortillas as support for the lettuce wraps, or double up the lettuce. You can also just eat with lettuce as pictured here or pack the ingredients separated in one container or in individual containers for a lunch-on-the-go option.

"EXCUSE ME, YOU THINK I'M CHEAP?"
Mr. Green

GUNTHER'S FROSTY FLAKES DONUTS WITH CEREAL MILK ICING

SEASON 10, EP: 17-18

"The Last One & The One Where They Say Goodbye"

Everyone knows about Gunther's big crush on Rachel, but his Billy Idol "White Wedding" hairdo isn't getting him noticed. Not only is he insanely jealous, he can't seem to keep the other friends straight. Is he flakey, yeah, but he's also frosty when it comes to anybody else who likes Rachel. We think this donut combo, inspired by Gunther's endless love, strikes just the right balance between the two.

DIFFICULTY: Hard
YIELD: 18 to 24 mini donuts
PREP & COOK TIME: 1 hour, plus 1 hour 40 minutes to proof

CEREAL MILK ICING AND TOPPING:

3 tablespoons Cereal & Cookie Milk made with frosty flake cereal (page 32)

2 cups powdered sugar, plus more as needed

1½ cups frosty flake cereal

FOR THE DONUTS:

2 tablespoons warm water (110°F to 115°F)

¾ cup plus 2 tablespoons warm milk (110°F to 115°F)

2¼ teaspoons active dry yeast

2 tablespoons granulated sugar

2¼ cups bread flour, plus more as needed

¾ cup all-purpose flour, plus ¼ cup for kneading and rolling

1 large egg, plus 1 egg yolk

¼ teaspoon freshly grated nutmeg

1 teaspoon vanilla extract

1 tablespoon malted milk powder

1½ teaspoons baking powder

¼ cup plus 2 tablespoons butter-flavored shortening, at room temperature

1 teaspoon salt

4 to 6 cups high smoke point vegetable oil (see notes on fry station, page 23)

TO MAKE THE ICING AND TOPPING: In a medium bowl, whisk the cereal milk into the powdered sugar. It will start out looking very pasty and then look thick, white, and glue-like. The consistency should be thick, yet creamy enough to dip donuts in. Adjust the consistency as needed by adding more cereal milk and test on a donut before glazing all of them.

Place 1 cup of the cereal in a large resealable plastic bag. Roll a rolling pin over the cereal to crush it. Reserve ½ cup of whole pieces of cereal as garnish.

TO MAKE THE DONUTS: In a small bowl, add the warm water and sprinkle the yeast on top. Stir in the sugar and let rest for up to 5 minutes, until it foams on top. If the yeast doesn't foam, it might be dead. Wait 5 more minutes. If there is no action, start over using fresh yeast.

Transfer the yeast mixture to the bowl of a stand mixer fitted with the dough hook, or to a medium bowl if mixing by hand. Add the bread flour and all-purpose flour. Add the egg and egg yolk, nutmeg, vanilla, malted milk powder, and baking powder and knead for 5 minutes on medium-low speed. Slowly add the shortening, while kneading. Add the salt. Continue to knead for 10 minutes on medium speed. If necessary, stop the mixer and scrape down the sides of the bowl. If the dough is sticking to the bottom and sides of the bowl, raise the speed and add 1 tablespoon of bread flour. Continue to knead for another 10 minutes. The dough should release from the sides of the bowl and cling to the hook in the final stages of kneading.

Transfer the dough to a clean work surface and form into a smooth ball by tucking the sides underneath and kneading and rocking it by hand. Transfer the dough to a lightly oiled bowl large enough to allow the dough to double in size. Cover with plastic wrap and use tape or a marker to mark on top of the plastic wrap indicating the size of the dough. Let the dough rise in a draft-free area until doubled in size, 30 to 40 minutes. Turn the dough out

Continued on page 136

Continued from page 135

on a lightly floured work surface, punch down the dough, and knead into a loose rectangle. Line a sheet tray with parchment paper or a silicone baking mat. Roll out the dough to ¼ inch thick or slightly less to account for the dough contracting.

To cut the donuts, use a 3½-inch donut cutter (with stabilized center hole cutter). Place each cut donut on the prepared sheet tray. Gather the dough scraps and reroll them until all the donuts are cut. (If the dough is difficult to work with while cutting, place it on a sheet tray and refrigerate for 10 minutes.) Let the cut donuts proof, covered with a clean lint-free kitchen towel or plastic wrap, at room temperature for 45 minutes to 1 hour.

To check if the donut dough is ready, poke it with a finger. If the dough slightly indents without quickly springing back, it's ready.

Prepare 2 sheet trays with several layers of paper towels. Set aside near the fry area. Fill a large pot two-thirds full with the oil. The oil should be deep enough to submerge the donuts. Heat over medium heat until the oil registers 365°F on a deep-fry thermometer. Use a skimmer to carefully slide a couple donuts into the oil. Cook until golden brown and cooked through, about 30 seconds per side. Use the skimmer to flip the donuts. Cook the other side. Remove the cooked donuts and place on paper towels to absorb the oil. Move donuts to wire racks to cool. Repeat this process with the remaining donuts.

To glaze the donuts, place the cereal milk icing in a shallow bowl that is big enough to dip the donut. Dip one side of a warm, not hot, donut into the cereal milk icing, turn it clockwise, and lift the donut so the excess glaze runs back into the bowl. Place the iced donuts on cooling racks with parchment paper and a sheet tray underneath. Immediately sprinkle with crushed and whole frosty flake cereal. These are best eaten the same day they're made.

NOTE: To substitute butter for the shortening, use 6½ tablespoons or 3¼ ounces of high-fat butter (82% or greater fat content).

> "RACHEL, I KNOW YOU'RE LEAVING TONIGHT, BUT I JUST HAVE TO TELL YOU. **I LOVE YOU.**"
> Gunther

ROSS'S "BROWNED" BUTTER AND TOASTED MARSHMALLOW CRISPIES

In an attempt to get tan, Ross goes to a tanning salon for the first time. Hilarity ensues when his PhD doesn't help him operate the tanning booth. He ends up extra-toasty dark on one side and ghostly white on the other. These childhood-favorite crispy marshmallow treats have nutty-flavored brown butter and a toasted marshmallow topping. It's like a delicious snack version of Ross's tanning-booth fiasco.

DIFFICULTY: Easy
YIELD: 1 serving
PREP & COOK TIME: 20 minutes

2 tablespoons butter, plus more for greasing the pan
½ cup mini marshmallows, plus ½ cup
½ teaspoon kosher salt
1 teaspoon almond extract
⅛ teaspoon ground cinnamon
1 cup crispy rice cereal

Butter a 3-by-5½-inch heatproof glass dish.

In a medium saucepan over medium heat, brown the butter, cooking and stirring until the butter foams up and the milk solids begin to caramelize, about 6 minutes. Be careful not to burn the butter. Remove from the heat. Add ½ cup of marshmallows and stir. Return to the stovetop and stir while cooking over medium heat until melted. Add the salt, almond extract, and cinnamon. Stir to combine. Stir in the cereal. Remove from the heat.

Press the mixture into the prepared dish and smooth the top by pressing it with a spatula. Set aside.

Unmold the rice crispy treat. Place a sheet tray on the stove or a heatproof surface and transfer the rice crispy treat to the sheet tray. Top the rice crispy treat with the remaining ½ cup of mini marshmallows, spreading them evenly. Use a kitchen torch to toast the marshmallows to a nice golden brown (or use extra-long fireplace matches).

Serve immediately or place in a covered plastic container to take on the go.

CHANDLER'S NEW YORK CHEESECAKE SQUARES

SEASON 1, EP: 7

"The One With the Blackout"

These decadent, frozen grab-and-go cheesecake bars pay homage to the many cheesy pickup lines Chandler employs throughout the series. True to form, Chandler seems to get a brain freeze when he can't find the right words to impress lingerie model Jill Goodacre during the blackout. Or there was that time that he couldn't find the words to stop Joanna from leaving him in a compromising position at the office. And, then there are times it would be better if he didn't think of something to say at all.

DIFFICULTY: Medium
YIELD: 8 squares
PREP & COOK TIME: 2½ hours, plus one hour to freeze

FOR THE CHEESECAKE BASE:
Unsalted butter, for greasing the ramekin
4 ounces cream cheese, at room temperature
¼ cup sour cream
3 tablespoons plus 1½ teaspoons powdered sugar
⅛ teaspoon kosher salt
1 large egg
⅛ teaspoon vanilla extract
1 tablespoon lemon juice
Zest of 1 medium lemon
3 tablespoons all-purpose flour

FOR THE ICE CREAM:
One 8-ounce package cream cheese, at room temperature, but not warm
1 cup sour cream, divided
One 12-ounce can evaporated milk
1½ cups heavy cream
1¼ cups granulated sugar
3 tablespoons lemon juice

8 graham crackers, plus more in case of breakage

Preheat the oven to 400°F.

TO MAKE THE CHEESECAKE BASE: Line an 8-ounce ramekin with a piece of parchment paper greased with butter. Carefully push down and pleat the side of the paper so it will fit neatly in the ramekin. Fold any overhanging paper down over the outside of the ramekin.

In the bowl of a stand mixer fitted with the paddle attachment, or in a medium bowl using a handheld mixer, cream the cream cheese. Mix on medium-high until smooth and creamy with no lumps, about 8 minutes. Add the sour cream, a couple of tablespoons at a time while mixing, until fully incorporated.

Add the powdered sugar and salt while beating. Switch to the whisk attachment and whisk in the egg. Add the vanilla, lemon juice, and lemon zest and continue to whisk until combined. Whisk in 2 tablespoons of the flour. Stop the mixer and scrape down the bottom and sides of the bowl. Remove the bowl from the stand mixer. Add the remaining 1 tablespoon of flour and stir until just combined.

Pour the batter into the prepared ramekin. Trim any excess parchment paper, leaving at least 2 inches above the rim. Place the ramekin on a sheet tray and bake until the center is slightly bouncy and the top souffléed with a dark caramel brown crust, 35 to 45 minutes. The cheesecake will deflate as it begins to cool. Wait 10 minutes, remove from the ramekin, and let rest with the paper on a wire rack until cool enough to touch. Slice the cheesecake and cut into ¼-inch cubes. Chill the cubes in a plastic bag or covered container in the refrigerator. The cubes can be made up to 2 days in advance and stored in a tightly covered container in the refrigerator.

Continued on page 140

Continued from page 139

TO MAKE THE ICE CREAM: In the bowl of a stand mixer fitted with the paddle attachment, or in a medium bowl using a handheld mixer, cream the cream cheese until no lumps are visible. Slowly add the sour cream in 3 additions, whisking to incorporate after each addition.

In a pitcher, stir together the evaporated milk, cream, and granulated sugar until the sugar is dissolved. Slowly add the milk mixture to the cream cheese mixture. Whisk to combine. Scrape down the sides and bottom of the bowl with a spatula. Stir in the lemon juice. Transfer to an ice cream maker and follow the manufacturer instructions to make the ice cream.

When the ice cream has thickened and is almost ready, slowly add in the diced cheesecake. Mix until thoroughly combined. Transfer the ice cream barrel to the freezer for 30 minutes, or until hard, if using the same day. Or pack tightly in a container topped with a piece of parchment. Cover and freeze for up to 5 days.

Line a sheet tray with parchment paper. Break the graham crackers in half, creating 2 squares. Each cheesecake bar will have a top and bottom cracker. Lay the bottom square out on the sheet tray. Scoop two scoops of ice cream on top of 1 square. Add a top graham cracker and carefully push down to flatten the ice cream to 1½ inches high. Alternatively, use a piece of waxed paper or plastic wrap to push down the ice cream, then top with a graham cracker. Use an offset spatula, or some waxed paper, to press and even out the sides. Remove any extra ice cream on the graham cracker with a paper towel and place the bars in an uncovered container or on a sheet tray in the freezer. Repeat with the remaining graham cracker squares. Make all the bars and freeze, uncovered, for 1 hour before eating. Once frozen, the bars can be sliced and quartered with a sharp knife to make mini bites. The bars taste best the day they are made; however, they can be individually wrapped in parchment paper and stored in a covered container in the freezer for up to 7 days. Use a sticker or masking tape to secure the paper around the ice cream.

"GUM WOULD BE PERFECTION."
Chandler

PETE'S KILLER FINANCIER CAKES

Monica's millionaire boyfriend, Pete, becomes an "ultimate fighter," or at least that's his plan. It's not quite as easy as he thinks, and his first fight almost kills him. Even though he hires a paid assassin, or "house painter," to help him win, he still ends up black and blue with more than a few "raspberries." While becoming an ultimate fighter may not be that easy, these almond, brown butter, raspberry, and blueberry cake bars are pure gold! Like anything new, they can be a little tricky at first, but are worth practicing and perfecting as they taste like a million bucks.

DIFFICULTY: Medium
YIELD: 10 to 12 cakes
PREP & COOK TIME: 25 minutes

½ cup plus 2 tablespoons unsalted butter, plus more for greasing mold

¾ cup almond meal or flour (fresh finely ground blanched almonds will also work)

¾ cup granulated sugar

¼ cup plus 2½ tablespoons all-purpose flour

¾ teaspoon salt

3 large egg whites

2 tablespoons powdered sugar

1 teaspoon vanilla extract or paste

10 to 12 raspberries or a combination of raspberries and blueberries

FUN FACT: The name *financier*, or *Bankers' Cake*, is said to derive from the traditional rectangular mold used to bake the small cakes, which resemble a bar of gold. They can also be baked in a cupcake pan.

Preheat the oven to 425°F. Butter a financier mold or spray with oil, place on a sheet tray, and set aside.

In a medium saucepan over medium-high heat, brown the butter, cooking and stirring until the butter foams up and the milk solids begin to caramelize, about 6 minutes. Be careful not to burn the butter as the butter solids go from brown to black quickly. Immediately strain the solids from the butter. Keep the brown butter warm by pouring it into a large coffee thermos or reheat to warm in the microwave before adding to the dry ingredients. In a medium bowl, whisk together the almond meal, granulated sugar, flour, and salt. Make a well in the center of the flour mixture. Set aside.

In the bowl of a stand mixer fitted with the whisk attachment, or in a medium bowl using a handheld mixer, whisk the egg whites until foamy, about 1 minute. Whisk in the powdered sugar, about 1 minute. Add the egg mixture to the center of the flour mixture and slowly whisk by hand until the ingredients are well combined. Continue to mix for another minute.

Add the warm brown butter in a slow steady stream to the batter. Stop and stir if needed to incorporate the butter evenly. Stir in the vanilla. Continue to mix and scrape the sides of the bowl until the ingredients are combined.

Transfer the batter to a large piping bag. Twist the opening to prevent the batter from spilling out the top. Snip off a small portion of the tip of the bag and squeeze the batter into the prepared mold. Fill each cup three-fourths full, leaving at least ⅛ inch at the top. Add a single raspberry to the center of each mold. Push the raspberry into the batter until just the very tip is showing.

Lower the oven temperature to 350°F and bake until the top edges of the cakes are golden brown and the cakes are cooked throughout, 20 to 25 minutes. A toothpick inserted into the center should come out clean. Rotate the pan once during baking for an even bake. Transfer the mold to a wire rack to cool slightly, then carefully unmold the cakes with an offset spatula. These are extra delicious warm and best consumed the day they're baked. They may also be stored in a covered container for 2 days in the refrigerator.

JOEY'S PEANUT BUTTER SPOON-SHAPED COOKIES & JAM

Joey loves peanut butter and jam, and he exudes a playful childish nature. Remember that time he wanted to add "peanut butter fingers" to Monica's wedding menu? And without thinking, he dove right in to taste Monica's scalding hot jam before it had cooled. Well, this invention of peanut butter cookie spoons and jam might end up being more popular than the Milk Master 2000. Joey can now keep his fingers out of the peanut butter jar and save his tongue from burning while pairing two of his favorite foods.

DIFFICULTY: Medium
YIELD: About 20 cookies, or 10 sandwich cookies
PREP & COOK TIME: 1 hour, plus 1 hour to freeze cream and batter

FOR THE COOKIES:
¼ cup unsalted butter, at room temperature
½ cup firmly packed dark brown sugar
⅓ cup powdered sugar
¾ cup creamy unsalted peanut butter
1 large egg
1 teaspoon vanilla extract
1 teaspoon molasses
1½ cups all-purpose flour, plus more for dusting
1½ teaspoons baking powder
½ teaspoon salt

FOR THE PEANUT BUTTER CREAM:
¼ cup unsalted butter, at room temperature
¼ cup plus 2 tablespoons creamy unsalted peanut butter
¼ cup plus 1 tablespoon powdered sugar
1 tablespoon heavy cream, plus more as needed

Strawberry jam, or another flavor, for topping

Preheat the oven to 350°F.

TO MAKE THE COOKIES: In the bowl of a stand mixer fitted with the paddle attachment, or in a medium bowl if using a handheld mixer, beat the butter until light and creamy, a few minutes. Switch to the whisk attachment. Add the brown sugar and powdered sugar and whisk until thoroughly combined. The dough will look dry and crumbly at first and then pull together. Add the peanut butter and whisk until combined. Beat in the egg, vanilla, and molasses.

In a separate medium bowl, whisk together the flour, baking powder, and salt with a fork. Add the flour mixture to the batter and whisk until combined.

Turn the dough out onto a piece of parchment paper. Press the dough into a 6-by-6-inch square. Wrap it tightly in plastic wrap and refrigerate for at least 30 minutes. Let the chilled dough rest at room temperature at least 10 minutes before rolling out. The dough should be pliable and not crack when rolling.

Line a sheet tray with parchment paper and set aside. Dust a separate sheet of parchment paper with flour. Add the dough on top and dust a little flour. Place another sheet of parchment paper on top of the dough. Using a rolling pin roll out the dough to ⅛ inch thick. Using a 4½-inch long teaspoon-shaped cookie cutter, cut out the cookies. Carefully transfer the cookies to the prepared sheet tray. Gather the scraps of dough, reroll, and cut out more cookies. If the spoons are not holding their shape, place the sheet tray in the freezer for 5 minutes to firm the dough. If any of the dough on the spoons has cracks, reroll until smooth.

The dough will hold its shape best if chilled before baking. Place a sheet tray of cut cookies in the freezer for 5 to 10 minutes to chill quickly before baking.

Continued on page 144

Continued from page 143

Bake the cookies until crisp and the edges have a subtle golden brown color, about 10 minutes. Let the cookies cool in the pan for 10 minutes, then carefully transfer to a wire rack to cool completely.

TO MAKE THE PEANUT BUTTER CREAM: In the bowl of a stand mixer fitted with the paddle attachment, or in a medium bowl if using a handheld mixer, cream the butter, a few minutes. Add the peanut butter and beat to combine. Switch to the whisk attachment. Add the powdered sugar and heavy cream and continue to whisk until light and creamy. Use the peanut butter cream immediately or, if it's too creamy to pipe, transfer the cream to a covered container and chill in the refrigerator for 30 minutes to 1 hour. The cream can be made 3 days ahead. Bring the cream to room temperature and whisk or stir vigorously until very creamy before using.

Place the cookies on a sheet tray. Add the peanut butter cream filling to a piping bag fitted with a star tip, or place it in a resealable plastic bag and cut ⅛ inch off one corner. Fill another piping bag (or resealable plastic bag) with jam. Just before serving, pipe a small amount of jam on the round portion of the spoon and then a small amount of the peanut butter cream on top. Assemble the decorated cookies on a serving tray and serve. Alternatively, serve the cookies with the peanut butter cream and jam on the side with a small serving knife. Or add a "peanut butter and jam spoon" to a bowl of vanilla ice cream. Yum!

NOTE: Double the filling recipe if using as a sweet dip for cookies.

"JAM, I LOVE JAM."

Joey

PHOEBE'S CHOCOLATE ESPRESSO "MUGGED" CAKE

SEASON 9, EP: 15

"The One With the Mugging"

Ross reveals a traumatic moment when his backpack, with his original artwork for his *Space Camp* comic book inside, was stolen. Phoebe soon realizes that she was in fact the scary kid who mugged him. This quick-and-easy chocolate espresso brownie cake is equivalent to a hug in a mug—conjuring up some delicious childhood memories, as long as they aren't about getting your space-camp book art stolen by street punk Phoebe.

Customize your mug: Make it a Joey mug by adding two "peanut butter fingers." Add smoked salt on top for Chandler; for Rachel, toffee or chocolate chip ice cream; for Monica, winter spices and whipped cream; and crushed chocolate sandwich cookies for Ross.

DIFFICULTY: Easy
YIELD: 1 mug cake (8- to 12-ounce mug)
PREP & COOK TIME: 10 minutes

4 tablespoons all-purpose flour
1 tablespoon unsweetened cocoa
1 teaspoon espresso powder
2½ tablespoons light brown sugar
¼ teaspoon baking powder
Pinch of salt
¼ cup milk
1 tablespoon vegetable oil or mild-flavored coconut oil
⅛ teaspoon vanilla extract
1 tablespoon dark chocolate chips
1 tablespoon crunchy unsweetened peanut butter
Vanilla ice cream or Whipped Cream (page 35), for serving

In an 8- to 12-ounce microwave-safe coffee mug, stir together the flour, cocoa, espresso powder, brown sugar, baking powder, and salt. Add the milk, oil, and vanilla to the mug and stir until the mixture is smooth and completely mixed. Add the chocolate chips and peanut butter to the center of the batter by scraping peanut butter off of one spoon with another spoon into the batter. Cook in the microwave on high heat until cooked throughout, 1 minute to 1 minute and 12 seconds. Let cool slightly, then top with a generous scoop of ice cream, whipped cream, or both. The dry ingredients can be premeasured and placed in a container or resealable plastic bag to make at the office (as long as there is a microwave). Just add 1 tablespoon of coconut oil and a ¼ cup of shelf-stable milk (sold in small cartons that don't need to be refrigerated). Coconut oil can be purchased in a box of ½-ounce packets.

EMILY'S EARL GREY SHORTBREAD COOKIES

Ross decides to shorten his engagement to Emily and marry her sooner than planned, but it's not long before Emily banishes him to the doghouse. Perhaps a short engagement was a bit hasty. These clever treats, flavored with Earl Grey tea, are delicious and definitely a better incentive than being put on a short leash. If only Emily knew Ross had a bit of a sweet tooth.

DIFFICULTY: Easy
YIELD: Twenty 3-inch cookies
PREP & COOK TIME: 1 hour 15 minutes

FOR THE GLAZE:

3 Earl Grey tea bags (about 3 teaspoons of tea)
¼ cup powdered sugar, plus more as needed
1½ teaspoons brewed Earl Grey tea

FOR THE COOKIES:

¼ cup powdered sugar
1½ tablespoons light brown sugar
¼ teaspoon kosher salt
1½ cups all-purpose flour
10 tablespoons unsalted butter, at room temperature
½ teaspoon orange zest
1 teaspoon vanilla extract

TO MAKE THE GLAZE: In a small mug, heat ¼ cup of water in the microwave. Add the tea bags and let steep, covered, 20 minutes. Remove the bags and reserve 1 teaspoon of the tea. Sift the powdered sugar and combine with the brewed tea in a small bowl. Add more sugar if needed. The glaze will be thin, but it should be thick enough to adhere to the baked cookies. Set aside.

TO MAKE THE COOKIES: Add the powdered sugar, brown sugar, salt, and flour to a food processor and pulse to combine and break up any lumps. Add the butter, a few tablespoons at time, with the motor running. Add the orange zest and vanilla, and 1 teaspoon of brewed tea. Pulse until thoroughly combined.

Preheat the oven to 300°F. Line a sheet tray with parchment paper or a silicone baking mat.

Transfer the dough to a sheet of parchment paper. Form the dough into a rectangle and roll out to ⅛ inch thick. Fold the dough over 1 or 2 times, and roll into a ¼-inch-thick rectangle. Using a 3-inch bone-shaped cookie cutter, cut out 20 bone shapes. Gather the scraps of dough, reroll, and cut out more cookies. Transfer the cookies to the prepared sheet tray. Use a chopstick or skewer to poke a row of 3 shallow 1/16-inch holes along the center of the bones. Don't push all the way through the dough. Bake until the edges have just a hint of light brown and the cookies are firm, 40 to 50 minutes. Let cool, then glaze.

ROSS'S TIERED WEDDING CAKE POPS

SEASON 4, EP: 24

"The One With Ross's Wedding, Part 2"

These delicious grab-and-go coconut-flavored cake pops have three tiers—one for each of Ross's wives: Carol, Emily, and Rachel. The bite-size tiers are dipped in tempered white chocolate and decorated like mini wedding cakes. Making these pops is a bit of a commitment, or labor of *love*, if you will. However, we added a few shortcuts and used a boxed cake mix with some added flavoring to speed up your trip down the aisle.

DIFFICULTY: Hard
YIELD: 15 cake pops
PREP & COOK TIME: 6 to 8 hours, plus 4 hours to chill

FOR THE FROSTING:
- ½ cup unsalted butter, at room temperature
- 1 cup powdered sugar, sifted
- 2 teaspoons coconut extract
- 1 teaspoon vanilla extract
- 2 tablespoon lite coconut milk, plus 1 teaspoon if needed

FOR THE CAKE:
- 1 box white cake or butter cake mix
- 1 teaspoon coconut extract
- ½ teaspoon vanilla extract

FOR THE CHOCOLATE COATING:
- 2 pounds couverture white chocolate chips, callets, or bars cut into small chips, divided
- 2 tablespoons coconut oil or vegetable oil, as needed to thin chocolate

FOR THE DECORATIONS (OPTIONAL):
- 6 ounces white nonpareils sprinkles
- 5 ounces sugar pearls
- 5¼ ounces pearlized gold or silver sugar sprinkles
- 15 store-bought mini fondant flowers

Fifteen 4½-inch wooden or candy sticks

TO MAKE THE FROSTING: In the bowl of a stand mixer fitted with the paddle attachment, or in a medium bowl if using a handheld mixer, cream the butter, a few minutes. Switch to the whisk attachment and add the powdered sugar. Whisk until combined. Add the coconut and vanilla extracts and the coconut milk, and whisk until creamy, 5 to 10 minutes. If the frosting is more stiff than creamy, add 1 teaspoon of coconut milk and whisk until creamy. The frosting can be made several days in advance and stored in an airtight container in the refrigerator. Let the frosting come to room temperature and whisk until creamy before using. The recipe may make slightly more frosting than needed for the cake pops, depending on the brand of cake mix.

TO MAKE THE CAKE: Follow the package directions to make the batter, then add the coconut extract and vanilla to the batter before baking. Bake three 9-inch round cakes. Let cool. Cakes can be wrapped and stored at room temperature overnight.

Line a sheet tray with parchment paper. Unwrap the cakes and trim any hard crust from the cakes. Transfer half of the cake to the bowl of a stand mixer fitted with the whisk attachment, or to a medium bowl if using a handheld mixer. Whisk on medium until the cake is broken down into ¼-inch pieces. Add the remaining cake in 2 sections and continue to whisk until the cake turns mostly to crumb. Break up any larger pieces with your hands. Add 3 to 4 tablespoons of the frosting, or more if needed. Mix until combined. The cake crumb should hold its shape when pressed between two fingers. If the mixture is dry, add another tablespoon of frosting and continue mixing until the cake mixture is ready.

TO ASSEMBLE THE TIERED CAKE POPS: Roll out the cake mixture between 2 pieces of parchment paper to ¼ inch thick, or press it into a sheet tray lined with parchment paper to ¼ inch thick. Use a 2-inch cookie cutter to cut out 15 rounds. Use a 1½-inch cookie cutter to cut out 15 rounds and set each one on top of a 2-inch round. Use a 1-inch cookie cutter to cut out 15 rounds to set on top of the others. Make room in the freezer for cake pops with sticks.

In a small microwave-safe bowl, melt 1 tablespoon of the white chocolate chips in the microwave on medium heat for 10 to 20 seconds, or until melted. Dip a stick into the melted chocolate and insert the stick into the top layer (the smallest tier) of one of the tiered cakes. Push the stick down through the center of each layer, but not through the bottom. Place the skewered cake pop on a sheet tray. Repeat with the remaining sticks and cakes. Place the sheet tray in the freezer for 4 hours until hard, or overnight.

TO MAKE THE CHOCOLATE COATING: Have an instant-read thermometer nearby. Set up a double boiler with a large pot. Have a second, slightly smaller pot selected that will fit on top of the large pot. Fill the bottom pot with several inches of water and heat the water to a boil, without the top pot, over medium heat. Set up a cutting board near the stovetop. Add a folded kitchen towel on top of the cutting board as a workstation.

Divide the remaining chocolate into two equal amounts (16 ounces each). Now divide one batch into 75% to melt (12 ounces) and 25% to "seed" (4 ounces). This is an important step, especially if you have never tempered chocolate before. Use this batch to decorate half of the cake pops.

Continued on page 150

Continued from page 149

TO MELT THE CHOCOLATE: Immediately place 75% (12 ounces) of the chocolate chips in the top pot or bowl and set it over the bottom pot of boiled water. Make sure the pot fits snugly so steam doesn't escape from the lower pot. Water coming into contact with the chocolate will cause the chocolate to seize up, making it unusable. Stir the chocolate continuously with a rubber spatula until the chocolate is almost all melted and the temperature is between 110°F to 113°F.

Immediately begin cooling the chocolate by seeding in more chips from the 25% reserved. Add a few chips at a time to the melted chocolate while stirring. Lift the pot of chocolate off the heat while continuing to stir. Move the pot of melted chocolate onto the kitchen towel on the cutting board. Turn off the heat under the double boiler. Check the temperature of the chocolate often while stirring and seeding in more chips. The temperature should hold at 86°F while seeding in the chocolate but never ever go lower than 79°F or higher than 86°F or the temper will break. If the temperature is in the range and there are a few chips not melted remove them from the chocolate with a spoon. If the chocolate is still melting and the 25% seeding chocolates are all gone, use some from the reserved half and continue to seed and stir until the chocolate is holding in the temperature range and new chips stop melting.

TEST THE CHOCOLATE: It should be smooth and liquid enough to dip the cake pops. It will have a ribbon effect that holds on top for a few seconds when a spatula is lifted from the chocolate. Spread a small amount of chocolate on a piece of parchment paper. Let is sit for 5 minutes. If it's shiny and beginning to noticeably harden, then it is tempered.

Maintain the melted chocolate temperature between 79°F and 86°F throughout the decorating process.

Stir in 1 teaspoon of coconut oil if the chocolate is too thick to work with. Leave the bottom pot on the stove as the chocolate will need to be warmed during the coating process and the temperature range maintained throughout. Heat the water if needed.

Line a sheet tray with waxed paper. To dip the first half of the cake pops, carefully tip the pot of chocolate, creating a deep pool of chocolate on one side. Remove a cake pop from the freezer. Hold the stick perpendicular above the pooled chocolate. The base of the cake will be the farthest from you. Dunk the cake pop into the chocolate and slowly roll it 360 degrees until it is fully submerged and covered in chocolate. Tip the stick down slightly to let the chocolate coat ⅛ inch of the stick, which helps secure the cake pop stick to the top of the cake. Lift up the cake, with the bottom layer above the pool of chocolate. Holding the stick with two fingers, gently twirl the cake from one side to the other. (If the chocolate is setting too quickly and not flowing down the cake sides, it might need to be warmed. Place the chocolate back on the double broiler, without turning on the heat, letting the residual heat from the warm water melt the chocolate. Don't heat the chocolate above 86°F or let it get colder than 79°F, or you will break the temper.) Gently scrape off any excess chocolate from the bottom layer of the cake pop after dipping with an offset spatula or paring knife while still warm. Place the cake pops on a sheet tray lined with waxed paper. Repeat until all the pops are all coated.

TO DECORATE THE CAKE POPS: Add some sprinkles to the sides of the bottom layer cake, or sprinkle over the whole cake pop. Place some remaining tempered chocolate into a piping bag with a #2 tip. The chocolate should be thick enough to hold some shape. If it's too thin, wait until it cools slightly. Use the chocolate to adhere nonpareils, sugar pearls, fondant flowers, and sprinkles to the cake pops. The cake pops can be left out for 1 day if they have a good seal of chocolate throughout, where the stick is inserted and on the bottom. They can also be frozen and stored covered. Let them come to room temperature in the refrigerator before serving.

TIP: Use a hair dryer on low heat to warm up the chocolate if it is getting hard and unmanageable during the decorating stage or while tempering. This will warm up the chocolate without breaking the temper.

ALL THE BALLS CHOCOLATE TRUFFLES

Monica's competitive spirit never seems to take a break, whether she is making holiday treats or playing a game of ball with the boys. These assorted dark and white chocolate truffles are nutty, sweet, and festive, and some are even filled with espresso. They won't stay in the air long, although just long enough to make it from your hand to your mouth. These truffles are best when using a high-quality baking couverture chocolate and heavy cream rather than milk or half-and-half.

DIFFICULTY: Easy
YIELD: About 20 truffles
PREP & COOK TIME: 2½ hours, plus 4 hours to chill

FOR THE DARK CHOCOLATE TRUFFLES:
8 ounces couverture bitter or semi-sweet baking
   chocolate
½ cup heavy cream
1 teaspoon unsalted butter, at room temperature

FOR THE WHITE CHOCOLATE TRUFFLES:
4 ounces couverture white baking chocolate
2 tablespoons heavy cream
1 teaspoon unsalted butter, at room temperature
1 teaspoon brown butter

FLAVORINGS PER ½ CUP GANACHE:
1 teaspoon vanilla extract
½ teaspoon coconut extract
1 teaspoon orange extract
1 tablespoon flavored liquor (optional)
1 tablespoon espresso powder

TOPPINGS:
⅔ cup unsweetened cocoa powder
½ cup finely chopped gourmet white chocolate or
   store-bought chocolate curls
½ cup chocolate jimmies
¾ cup finely chopped peanuts, almonds, and
   hazelnuts
½ cup malted milk powder

ACCENT FLAVOR SUGGESTIONS:
Flake sea salt
Citrus zest
Demerara sugar

TO MAKE THE DARK CHOCOLATE TRUFFLES: Chop the chocolate into small pieces. Transfer to a medium heatproof bowl. In a small saucepan over medium-low heat, or in a microwave-safe bowl in a microwave, heat the cream until simmering (almost boiling). Pour the cream over the chocolate pieces and let rest without stirring for 3 to 5 minutes. Use a spatula, not a whisk, to incorporate the chocolate and cream. Stir slowly and then raise the speed as the chocolate becomes dark and creamy like hot pudding. Add the butter and stir until completely melted. If making more than one flavor of truffle, divide the chocolate ganache evenly into separate bowls, with at least ½ cup of ganache in each bowl. Add a flavoring of choice (such as vanilla, coconut, orange, liqueur, or espresso powder) and stir to combine. Smooth out the top and place a piece of parchment paper or plastic wrap directly on top of the ganache. Transfer to the refrigerator and chill for 4 hours or overnight.

TO MAKE THE WHITE CHOCOLATE TRUFFLES: Chop the white chocolate into small pieces. Follow the instructions for the dark chocolate truffles, adding in the brown butter at the same time as the regular butter.

TO ASSEMBLE: Remove the ganache from the refrigerator. Place the desired toppings into separate bowls. Scoop out a small portion of ganache and roll it between the palm of your hands to make a 1-inch ball. Drop the ball into the desired topping and roll to coat. The weight of the ball will help the topping adhere. If using an accent flavor, incorporate it into the ganache before rolling or sprinkle the ball with the desired flavor. For instance, dry ingredients like salt can go in the ganache or be used as a topping, whereas orange zest is best incorporated into the truffle so it doesn't dry out. Repeat with the remaining balls. Store in an airtight container for up to 7 days.

RACHEL'S ICED BABY BUNNY COOKIES

Ross and Rachel's daughter Emma's first birthday party is off to a rocky start. Ross and Rachel are late, they get pulled over twice, and the bunny cake looks X-rated due to an order mix-up at the bakery. Bored and with their own plans, Chandler, Monica, Phoebe, and Joey decide to race windup toys to see who will have to stay until Rachel and Ross arrive. In the end, all turns out well as Ross transforms the phallic cake into a cute bunny and Emma blurts out that she is "one!" These perfectly sweet lemon and soothing lavender iced cookies will keep everybody calm at your next party.

DIFFICULTY: Medium
YIELD: About 20 cookies
PREP & COOK TIME: 2 hours, plus 30 minutes to chill

FOR THE COOKIE DOUGH:

1 cup unsalted butter, at room temperature
½ cup powdered sugar, sifted
½ cup granulated sugar
1 large egg
½ teaspoon lemon extract
1 teaspoon lemon zest
½ teaspoon lemon juice
2½ cups all-purpose flour, plus more for dusting
½ teaspoon salt
1 teaspoon culinary lavender (optional)

FOR THE ROYAL ICING:

4 tablespoons meringue powder (egg white powder)
¼ teaspoon cream of tartar
2 pounds powdered sugar, sifted, divided
1 teaspoon lemon extract
High-quality food coloring paste in assorted colors

Sprinkles (optional)

TO MAKE THE COOKIE DOUGH: In the bowl of a stand mixer fitted with the paddle attachment, or in a medium bowl if using a handheld mixer, cream the butter, for a few minutes. Add the powdered sugar and the granulated sugar and beat until light and fluffy, a few minutes. Add the egg, lemon extract, lemon zest, and lemon juice. Combine thoroughly. Beat in the flour, salt, and culinary lavender, if using. Mix until the dough pulls together and the flour is fully combined.

Transfer the dough to a sheet of parchment paper dusted with flour. Dust flour on top and top the dough with another piece of parchment paper. Using a rolling pin, roll into a ½-inch-thick rectangle. If the dough is very soft and the kitchen is very hot, wrap the dough with plastic, or place in a gallon-size plastic storage bag, and lay the dough flat on a sheet tray that will fit in the refrigerator or freezer. Chill the dough for 30 minutes in the refrigerator or for 10 minutes in the freezer to firm up.

Place a rack in the lower third of the oven and preheat the oven to 375°F. Line a sheet tray with parchment paper.

Transfer the dough to a lightly floured work surface. Let the dough rest until pliable, about 10 minutes, so that it can be rolled without cracking. Roll out to ¼ inch thick.

Using a 3½-inch bunny-shaped cookie cutter, cut out the cookies and transfer the cutouts to the prepared sheet tray. Leave ¼ inch between the cookies. Chill the cutouts in the refrigerator or freezer until firm. (If tightly wrapped, the cutouts can be frozen for up to 2 weeks. Bake them from frozen and add more time for baking if needed.)

Bake the cookies for 10 to 12 minutes, rotating the sheet tray halfway through baking to avoid uneven cooking. The cookies should be light golden brown on the bottom and pale, but firm on the top. Let the cookies cool on the sheet tray for 3 minutes before transferring them to a wire rack to cool completely before icing.

Continued on page 154

Continued from page 153

TO MAKE THE ROYAL ICING: In a medium bowl, whisk together the meringue powder and ¼ cup plus 3 tablespoons of water until fully combined. The mixture will be slightly foamy. Whisk in the cream of tartar. Strain the mixture into the bowl of a stand mixer fitted with the paddle attachment, or into a medium bowl if using a handheld mixer, removing any sediment. Add in half of the powdered sugar. Beat on low speed until the sugar is fully incorporated. Add more powdered sugar, a cup or two at a time, beating between additions and stopping the mixer occasionally to scrape down the bottom and sides of the bowl.

Continue beating the icing for 15 minutes, until it is thick and creamy enough to hold a stiff peak. Stir in the lemon extract. Transfer the icing to a covered container, or to several smaller containers if using multiple colors. Add additional warm water, 1 tablespoon at a time, to the icing to create the desired consistency for decorating the cookies. Use thinner icing for flooding the cookies and a stiffer icing for detail work and creating a border or "dam" at the edge of the cookie. Keep in mind it is easier to thin the icing than to thicken it. It will take a minute for the water to really settle in after mixing, so wait several minutes before adding any more water.

Test the icing by running a spoon through it. The icing should slowly merge back into a smooth texture within about 10 seconds of running a spoon through it. If the icing is too runny it will be difficult to control. If it's too stiff, it won't create a smooth finish and will be difficult to work with. Icing without any food coloring will last a couple of days. Store it covered, not in a piping bag, at room temperature.

TO DECORATE THE COOKIES: Add food coloring to the icing before adding to a piping bag, if using. Check the consistency of the icing before filling the piping bag. Fit a piping bag with a #2 tip, to outline the cookie (creating a dam), and #2 to #5 tip to flood the icing inside the dam. To fill the piping bag with icing, transfer it to a tall glass. Fold the tip to the side, so the icing doesn't leak out. Roll the top edge of the bag down over the outside of the glass and use a spatula to fill the bag with icing.

Pipe the dam first with #2 tip, then with a separate bag of icing fitted with a #5 tip, immediately pipe more icing into the dam to flood. Use a toothpick to remove any air bubbles and lightly tap and shake the bottom of the cookie on the work surface to smooth out the icing. Alternatively, dip the front of the cookie in icing. Let the excess icing run off back into the bowl. Immediately top with sprinkles, if using. Feel free to decorate your bunny cookies as cute as possible, which would surely make Rachel proud.

NOTE: Royal icing takes at least 24 hours to completely set. Colors will need to set completely before topping with another color.

MONICA'S GIANT CHOCOLATE CHIPPER/CHOPPER NUTTY COOKIES

Monica bumps into her high school crush, Chip, who owns a chopper motorcycle and has a giant ego. Monica, still clinging to some old feelings for him, awkwardly blurts out that his name is Chip and that his chopper is named Chipper. Eventually Monica tires of Chip, but that doesn't mean she would pass up a giant chocolate chip peanut butter skillet cookie inspired by Chip. Perhaps a little old-school comfort is just what she needs.

DIFFICULTY: Easy
YIELD: 4 cookies
PREP & COOK TIME: 40 minutes

¼ cup plus 2 tablespoons unsalted butter, at room temperature

¼ cup plus 2 tablespoons firmly packed dark brown sugar

¼ cup plus 2 tablespoons granulated sugar

1 large egg

2 tablespoons unsweetened, unsalted peanut butter

2 tablespoons coconut oil

1 teaspoon vanilla extract

1 cup plus 2 tablespoons all-purpose flour

1½ tablespoons buckwheat flour

½ teaspoon baking soda

¼ teaspoon salt

½ cup assorted chopped nuts, such as walnuts, peanuts, hazelnuts, and Brazil nuts

½ cup dark chocolate chips (60% cacao)

⅛ teaspoon Maldon sea salt, for garnish

Vanilla ice cream (optional), for serving

Preheat the oven to 350°F.

In the bowl of a stand mixer fitted with the paddle attachment, or in a medium bowl if using a handheld mixer, cream the butter, brown sugar, and granulated sugar, until the butter is creamy and the sugar is fully incorporated, a few minutes. Mix in the egg. Then add the peanut butter, coconut oil, and vanilla and beat until fully combined.

In a small bowl, stir together the all-purpose flour, buckwheat flour, baking soda, and salt. Add half the flour mixture into the wet ingredients and mix until incorporated. Repeat with the remaining flour mixture. Stir in the nuts and chocolate chips.

Grease a 6-inch cast-iron skillet with butter or coconut oil. Transfer ½ cup of dough to the skillet and press down to fill the skillet. Bake until the center is set, about 20 minutes. Sprinkle the cookie with the sea salt. Repeat with the remaining batter to make 4 cookies total. The remaining dough can be baked in a cooled skillet. Or portion out the dough, tightly wrap in plastic wrap, and freeze. Let the dough come to room temp before baking.

Let the cookie cool slightly and serve in the skillet with a scoop of vanilla ice cream on top, if using. Or, carefully remove cookie, let cool on a wire rack, and wrap in foil for a grab-and-go snack.

PHOEBE'S EGGNOG FRUIT TARTS

Phoebe makes a huge decision to be a surrogate mother for her brother Frank and his wife who can't have their own children. At the doctor's office, Frank excitedly blurts out to the doctor, "Go get the eggs and put them in there!" That's also not bad advice when it comes to holiday desserts. These rich and creamy eggnog-flavored custard tarts with a crisp cookie crust are a crowd favorite. Top them with seasonal fruit and serve for family and friends at any holiday meal.

DIFFICULTY: Hard
YIELD: One 10-inch tart shell, or 8 to 10 smaller tart shells
PREP & COOK TIME: 2½ hours, plus 4 hours to set

FOR THE TART SHELLS:
Rachel's Iced Baby Bunny Cookies dough (page 153)
1 teaspoon vanilla extract
¼ teaspoon freshly grated nutmeg
Pinch of ground cinnamon

FOR THE EGGNOG CREAM
3 large egg yolks
¼ cup plus 1 tablespoon granulated sugar
3 tablespoons cornstarch, sifted
1 cup milk
1 tablespoon light brown sugar (break up any lumps)
½ cup heavy cream
½ inch vanilla bean, split and scraped, or 1 teaspoon vanilla extract
¾ teaspoon freshly grated nutmeg
Pinch of allspice
2 tablespoons rum, brandy, or bourbon
1½ tablespoons unsalted butter

FOR SERVING:
1 cup fresh berries
½ cup assorted fruit, sliced
½ cup apricot jam

TO MAKE THE TART SHELLS: Prepare the Iced Baby Bunny Cookies dough as instructed on page 153, replacing the lemon extract, lemon juice, and culinary lavender in the recipe with the vanilla extract, nutmeg, and cinnamon to the recipe.

Preheat oven to 350°F.

On a clean work surface, roll the dough to ⅛ inch thick. If making one tart, using a 10-inch round or fluted tart mold as a guide, cut out a round of dough, with enough excess dough to cover the bottom and sides of the mold. Transfer the round to the mold and press into place. Trim the edge with a paring knife. Place the mold on a sheet tray and chill until hard in the refrigerator or freezer, about 30 minutes in the refrigerator and 10 to 15 minutes in the freezer.

If making small tarts, follow the same process, using a round or fluted tart mold as a guide, and cut out 8 to 10 rounds of dough. Reroll any excess trimmed dough and make more tarts, as needed, until all the dough is cut.

To cook the tart shells, place the tart on a sheet tray. Cover the tart(s) with parchment paper. Use individual pieces of paper for the smaller tarts. Place pie weights on top of the paper to hold the dough shape while the tart(s) bake. Bake for 20 minutes, then rotate the tray. Bake for another 5 to 10 minutes. Remove from the oven and carefully remove the hot weights and parchment paper. Reduce oven heat to 300°F and cook, uncovered, until the edges are golden and the center is fully cooked like a cookie, about 5 minutes. Let the tart(s) cool in the mold on a wire rack.

TO MAKE THE EGGNOG CREAM: In the bowl of a stand mixer fitted with the whisk attachment, or in a medium bowl if using a handheld mixer, combine the egg yolks and granulated sugar. Whisk until the eggs lighten and thicken enough to create a ribbon effect on the top layer after lifting up the whisk, about 3 to 5 minutes. Sprinkle in the cornstarch and whisk until thoroughly combined. Set aside.

Continued on page 158

Continued from page 157

Before cooking the eggnog cream, set up a bowl filled with ice, and set another bowl on top of the ice. You'll use the top bowl to quickly cool the hot eggnog cream after cooking. Have a fine-mesh strainer nearby.

In a medium saucepan over medium heat, warm the milk. Whisk in the brown sugar, cream, vanilla bean (if using vanilla extract, wait until just before straining before adding), nutmeg, and allspice and whisk continuously while cooking. Bring to a boil and reduce the heat to low and simmer.

Slowly whisk one-fourth of the hot milk mixture in with the beaten eggs. (This tempering process keeps the yolks from scrambling when you add them back with the rest of the simmering milk by limiting the amount of hot liquid being included at one time.)

Pour the tempered eggs into the saucepan with the remaining hot milk. Heat over medium heat, while whisking, until the eggnog cream boils. Cook until the eggnog cream is thick and bubbly in the center, 3 to 5 minutes, or until the custard is thick enough to coat a spoon. Stir in the rum. If using vanilla extract, stir in now. Remove the saucepan from the heat.

Immediately pour the hot eggnog cream through a fine-mesh strainer into the bowl sitting over the bowl of ice and use a spatula to push through any thickened cream. Remove the vanilla bean, if using. Add the butter to the bowl and whisk into the eggnog cream. Stir until it is slightly cooled. Place plastic wrap directly on top (lightly pressing into cream) to prevent a skin from forming. Arrange the tart shell(s), still in the molds, on a sheet tray. Remove the plastic wrap from the eggnog cream and pour the warm (not hot) eggnog cream into the cooked tart shell(s). Smooth out the top and transfer the tarts to the refrigerator to cool overnight, or at least 4 hours. Carefully unmold the chilled tarts and place them on a sheet tray.

TO SERVE: Top the tart(s) with the fresh berries and fruit. In a microwave-safe bowl, heat the jam with 1 tablespoon of water and microwave on high heat for 30 to 40 seconds. Strain any fruit chunks out. With a pastry brush, brush the jam on top of the fruit to keep them shiny and preserved.

ROSS & MARCEL'S FAMOUS MONKEY BARS

Ross's beloved pet monkey, Marcel, is missing. He's not at the zoo, and the janitor at the zoo says that Marcel didn't die, either, which is good news. Eventually Ross finds out that Marcel is famous and starring in movies and beer commercials. After reminiscing about some cute Marcel antics, like the "monkey raisins" he would leave in Rachel's hat, the friends plan a reunion. These decadent monkey bars include chocolate, caramel, banana chips, coconut, graham cracker crumbs, crunchy raw almonds, and a touch of flaky salt. Make a batch to share if you want to be the star of the party.

DIFFICULTY: Medium
YIELD: 20 bars
PREP & COOK TIME: 1½ hours, plus 8 hours to chill

FOR THE GRAHAM CRACKER BASE:

½ cup all-purpose flour
½ cup graham cracker crumbs
3 tablespoons unsalted butter, melted, plus more for greasing pan
½ cup firmly packed light brown sugar

FOR THE CRUNCHY MONKEY TOPPING:

½ cup toasted coconut flakes
4 ounces premium white baking chocolate, roughly chopped
¼ cup dried currants
½ cup sweetened banana chips, roughly chopped
½ cup raw almonds, roughly chopped
¼ teaspoon flaky sea salt
1 recipe Caramel Filling (page 35), freshly made and hot
1 ganache recipe from Richard & Monica's Toasted Meringue "Mustache" S'mores Bars (page 163)

TO MAKE THE GRAHAM CRACKER BASE: Preheat the oven to 350°F. Butter a 9-by-9-inch baking pan and layer 2 cut pieces of parchment paper so they cover the bottom and the sides of the pan. This will make the bars easier to remove from the pan when ready to serve.

In a medium bowl, mix together the flour, graham cracker crumbs, butter, and brown sugar. Transfer the mixture to the baking pan and tightly press down, creating an even layer on the bottom of the baking pan. Bake until set, 15 to 20 minutes. Cool completely.

TO MAKE THE CRUNCHY MONKEY TOPPING: In a medium bowl, combine the coconut flakes, white chocolate, currants, banana chips, almonds, and salt. Set aside.

Make the caramel filling once the graham base is cooled. Pour the hot caramel filling on top of the graham cookie base. The filling should be cool before starting the ganache.

Make the ganache. Immediately, pour the hot liquid ganache over the caramel and graham cracker base and use a spatula to spread it out until smooth. Immediately sprinkle the crunchy monkey topping evenly over the ganache. Let cool. Refrigerate, unconvered, overnight. Unmold the mixture from the pan by lifting up the parchment paper sides and transfer to a cutting board. Slice down the middle, creating two equal halves, and then slice the remaining halves into equal size monkey bars. Enjoy!

ROSS'S EVERYTHING'S UPSIDE-DOWN CAKES

SEASON 9, EP: 1

"The One Where No One Proposes"

Whether it's getting married on a whim in Las Vegas or saying the wrong name at the altar, it seems Ross is good at turning his life upside down. These mini cakes have a nutty flavor from the buckwheat and a sweet banana date topping, and they are perfect for dessert with vanilla ice cream or whipped cream. They're also just as delicious with your favorite hot brew in the morning. Cake for breakfast is our favorite version of upside-down cake.

DIFFICULTY: Medium
YIELD: 10 mini cakes
PREP & COOK TIME: 1½ hours

FOR THE BANANA DATE TOPPING:

1 large yellow banana
4 tablespoons unsalted butter
¼ cup muscovado sugar
¼ cup finely chopped seeded dates
⅛ teaspoon salt
½ teaspoon ground cinnamon
Pinch of freshly grated nutmeg
½ teaspoon vanilla extract
2 tablespoons heavy cream
2 tablespoons cake flour, plus more for dusting the pans

FOR THE CAKE BATTER:

1 cup plus 2 tablespoons cake flour
1½ tablespoons buckwheat flour
1 teaspoon baking powder
½ teaspoon baking soda
¼ teaspoon salt
¼ cup plus 2 tablespoons buttermilk, at room temperature
1 teaspoon vanilla extract
2 tablespoons rum
2 tablespoons plus 1½ teaspoons muscovado sugar
½ cup plus 2 tablespoon granulated sugar
2 large eggs, separated, at room temperature
6 tablespoons unsalted butter, at room temperature

Preheat the oven to 350°F. Spray ten 6-ounce ramekins, or jumbo muffin cups, with cooking oil and dust with flour.

TO MAKE THE BANANA DATE TOPPING: Peel the banana. Slice off and mash a three-fourths section of the banana and set aside. Cut the remaining one-fourth of the banana on the diagonal into ten ⅛-inch slices. Lay one slice in the center of each of the prepared ramekins

In a medium saucepan over medium-low heat, melt the butter. When the butter is melted, stir in the muscovado sugar, mashed banana, dates, salt, cinnamon, nutmeg, and vanilla. Use the back of a wooden spoon to mash the dates and banana while stirring the sauce so the sugar doesn't burn. Cook until the sugar and banana melt down into a thick sauce. Stir in the cream and mix until thoroughly combined. Sprinkle in the cake flour and stir. The mixture will resemble a thick sauce when ready.

Remove from the heat and let cool slightly. Spoon approximately 1 tablespoon of sauce into each ramekin on top of the banana slices. Smooth out the sauce so that it covers the bottom. The topping can be made 1 day in advance and stored in a covered container in the refrigerator. Warm the sauce slightly in a microwave oven, about 30 seconds, and stir before using.

TO MAKE THE CAKE BATTER: In a medium bowl, sift together the cake and buckwheat flours, baking powder, baking soda, and salt. In a glass pitcher, combine the buttermilk, vanilla, and rum. In a separate medium bowl, sift together the muscovado and granulated sugars, pushing through the larger pieces of sugar, and using your fingers to break down any sugar lumps. Set aside.

To make the meringue, in the bowl of a stand mixer fitted with the whisk attachment, or in a medium bowl if using a handheld mixer, whisk the egg whites to stiff peaks. Transfer the egg whites to a clean bowl and set aside. (See Chef Monica's tips for meringue on page 21.)

In a clean bowl of a stand mixer fitted with a clean whisk attachment, or in a medium bowl if using a handheld mixer, cream the butter until light and fluffy on medium speed, about 2 minutes. Slowly add the sifted sugars to the creamed butter and whisk until thoroughly combined, 2 to 3 minutes. Add the egg yolks, 1 at a time, beating well after each addition, until combined.

Alternate whisking in one-third of the flour mixture with one-third of the buttermilk mixture until the batter is just incorporated. Stop the mixer and scrape down the sides and bottom of bowl in between additions. Spoon in about ¼ cup of the egg whites into the batter and mix thoroughly. Carefully fold in the remaining egg whites using the stand mixer whisk as a hand whisk. Streaks of whites and some puff of whites will remain. Don't overmix and deflate the whites.

Scoop approximately ¼ cup of batter into the ramekins. Use a spoon or a spatula to smooth out the top of the batter.

Place ramekins directly on the center rack in the oven for even air flow, or on top of a sheet tray. Bake until the center of the cake springs back when pressed with a finger, or a toothpick inserted into the center comes out clean, 18 to 25 minutes. Check the cakes and rotate halfway through cooking if they are not baking evenly. (Cakes cooked in muffin cups cook a little hotter and quicker, so check for doneness at 15 minutes.)

Let the cakes cool for 5 minutes on a wire rack. To release the cakes from the ramekins, run a paring knife around the inner edge of the cakes, then carefully flip the cakes to release them. If any topping is in the ramekin or muffin cups, transfer it back to the top of the cakes. Let the cakes cool on a wire rack for 10 minutes before serving. They taste delicious warm after baking or heated in the microwave oven for a few seconds.

"WELL, I DIDN'T . . . I DIDN'T PROPOSE.
UNLESS . . . DID I? I HAVEN'T SLEPT IN 40 HOURS.
AND IT DOES SOUND LIKE SOMETHING I WOULD DO."

Ross

RICHARD & MONICA'S TOASTED MERINGUE "MUSTACHE" S'MORES BARS

Joey and Chandler are obsessed with all things Richard, Monica's handsome older boyfriend. Chandler grows a ridiculous mustache like Richard's, and Joey starts smoking cigars because Richard does. Monica becomes a little jealous as her friends spend more time with Richard than with her, so why wouldn't she craft a perfect "Richard-esque" dessert to compete! These decadent dark-chocolate ganache bars with a graham cracker base are topped with smoked salt and toasted meringue "mustaches."

DIFFICULTY: Medium
YIELD: 12 bars
PREP & COOK TIME: 2 to 3 hours, plus 8 hours to chill

FOR THE GRAHAM CRACKER BASE:

1½ cups graham cracker crumbs

¼ cup plus 1 tablespoon unsalted butter, melted

½ teaspoon baking powder

1 teaspoon vanilla extract

⅛ teaspoon salt

1 recipe Caramel Filling (page 35), freshly made and hot

FOR THE GANACHE TOPPING:

2 cups dark chocolate chips (60% cacao)

1½ cups heavy cream

1 teaspoon unsalted butter

FOR THE MERINGUE "MUSTACHE":

3 large egg whites

½ cup plus 2 tablespoons granulated sugar

TO MAKE THE GRAHAM CRACKER BASE: Preheat the oven to 350°F. Butter a 9-by-9-inch baking pan and layer 2 cut pieces of parchment paper so they cover the bottom and the sides of the pan. This will make the bars easier to remove from the pan after baking.

In a medium bowl, thoroughly combine the graham cracker crumbs, butter, baking powder, vanilla, and salt. Press the graham cracker base tightly into the pan, creating an even layer on just the bottom of the pan. Cover the base with parchment paper. Use a glass or the back of a spoon to smooth out the surface. Remove the parchment paper. Bake for 10 minutes. Let cool slightly in the pan on a wire rack for 10 minutes. Leave the oven at 350°F.

Make the caramel filling once the base has fully cooled, and immediately pour over the graham cracker base. Spread the mixture evenly and bake for 15 to 20 minutes, or until bubbled and caramelized on top. Cool down and then refrigerate uncovered until cold, about 20 minutes before making the ganache.

TO MAKE THE GANACHE TOPPING: Place the chocolate chips in a medium bowl. In a small saucepan over medium heat, or in a microwave-safe glass measuring pitcher in the microwave, heat the cream to a simmer (just below boiling). Pour the cream over the chocolate chips and let sit for 3 minutes. Use a spatula or spoon to slowly stir the cream into the chips. As the chocolate chips melt and the cream incorporates, the ganache will be thick, dark, and creamy like thin pudding. Stir in the butter and pour over the graham cracker and caramel filling base. Smooth the top of the ganache with an offset spatula. Tap the pan a few times on the counter to release any air bubbles in the ganache before chilling.

Continued on page 164

Continued from page 163

Let cool, then refrigerate, uncovered, at least 8 hours or until completely set.

To cut the bars, use a paring knife to release the ganache from the sides of the pan. Cover the top of the pan with a cutting board or sheet tray, flip it over, and tap on the bottom of the pan to unmold.

Turn the ganache right side up by placing a piece of parchment paper on the graham cracker base and topping it with a cutting board or sheet tray. Flip again, turning the ganache right side up.

Using a sharp chef's knife, cut down the center creating 2 equal halves, about 4½ by 9 inches each. Trim the sides and then slice 12 equal size bars, about 4 by 1½ inches each. Refrigerate in a covered container.

TO MAKE THE MERINGUE MUSTACHE: In a large stainless steel bowl, or in the bowl of a stand mixer fitted with the whisk attachment, whisk together the egg whites and sugar until combined. (See Chef Monica's meringue tips on page 21.)

Place the stand mixer bowl, or a medium-large heatproof bowl with the whisked egg whites on top of a medium saucepan filled one-fourth full with water, creating a double boiler. Bring the water to a simmer (just below boiling) over medium-high heat while whisking the eggs and sugar. Heat the mixture until it registers 160°F on an instant-read thermometer. Return the bowl to the stand mixer fitted with a whisk attachment, or pour the heated mixture into the stand mixer bowl. Whisk until the bowl is cool to touch and the meringue is thick, fluffy, and forms stiff peaks when the whisk is lifted.

Use a spatula to transfer the meringue to a piping bag fitted with a #30 closed star tip or French star pastry tip to pipe 12 of your own signature mustaches, perhaps with a handlebar lift at the end. Or transfer the meringue to a plastic bag and cut the corner off, then pipe the mustaches. Place each mustache on top of a single s'mores bar.

Arrange the bars on a sheet tray, on top of a heatproof surface. Use a kitchen torch to toast the mustaches, using short bursts of flame, to avoid melting the bars. Or, use an extra-long fireplace match to toast the mustaches. Blow out any mustaches that catch fire. Serve the bars immediately for the best flavor. The bars will last for 2 to 3 days stored in a covered container in the refrigerator.

"OH, WE FLIPPED FOR IT.
I GOT THE CIGAR AND
HE GOT THE MUSTACHE."
Joey

JOEY'S EMPTY BAG BROWNIES

Sometimes Joey has the best intentions, but his stomach gets the better of him. When he's dating Rachel, he shows up with a bouquet of lilies and a brownie. Well, not a brownie. Just a brown bag because he ate the brownie on the way home. But there's no sad empty bag here! These decadent brownies are topped with crispy puffed cocoa, adding an extra-chocolaty crunch. The dense rich chocolate fudgy filling and sweet hazelnuts inside might make these the best brownies you'll ever have. Or never have, if Joey gets to them first.

DIFFICULTY: Easy
YIELD: 9 large brownies
PREP & COOK TIME: 1½ hours

FOR THE CHOCOLATE BASE:

1 cup unsalted butter, plus more for greasing the pan
1 cup unsweetened Dutch cocoa powder
2 teaspoons espresso powder
2 tablespoons milk
1 tablespoon vegetable oil

FOR THE BATTER:

1½ cups all-purpose flour, plus more for dusting the pan
1 teaspoon salt
1 teaspoon baking powder
1 teaspoon cornstarch
4 large eggs
½ cup firmly packed light brown sugar
1¾ cups granulated sugar
1 teaspoon vanilla extract
1 cup dark chocolate chips (60% cacao)
¾ cup dry-roasted unsalted hazelnuts, or nut of your choice, chopped or smashed
2 cups puffed cocoa cereal

Preheat the oven to 375°F. Butter the baking pan and sprinkle with flour.

TO MAKE THE CHOCOLATE BASE: In a small saucepan over medium heat, melt the butter. Stir in the cocoa powder, espresso powder, milk, and vegetable oil. Remove from the heat and let cool.

TO MAKE THE BROWNIE BATTER: In a medium bowl, combine the flour, salt, baking powder, and cornstarch. In the bowl of a stand mixer fitted with the whisk attachment, or in a separate medium bowl if using a handheld mixer, whisk together the eggs, brown sugar, and granulated sugar until light and fluffy, a full 10 minutes. Whisk in the vanilla. Stop the mixer and scrape down the sides of the bowl. Pour in the cooled chocolate base and whisk until mostly incorporated. Remove the bowl from the stand mixer and stir in the flour mixture until just combined. Stir in ½ cup of chocolate chips and the nuts.

Pour the batter into the prepared pan. Smooth the top with a spatula. Bake for 35 minutes. Reduce the heat to 350°F and bake until the edges are crisp and firm, 10 to 15 minutes. The center will still have some give, but a tester should come out almost clean. Remove the pan and sprinkle the remaining ½ cup of chocolate chips on top. Place the pan back in the oven for 1 minute. Remove from the oven, and use a spatula to spread the melted chocolate chips in an even layer. Pour the puffed cocoa cereal on top and arrange in an even layer. Let the brownies cool on a wire rack for 2 hours before slicing. The brownies can be stored in an airtight container in the refrigerator for 2 days.

TIP: Cocoa cereal topping will degrade in the refrigerator from moisture. If you're not eating all the brownies in one day like Joey, skip the topping or warm the chocolate with a kitchen torch and add the topping before serving.

RACHEL'S APPLE CHAI MILK TEA LATTE CUPCAKES

SEASON 2, EP: 17

"The One Where Eddie Moves In"

Rachel's waitressing skills might need a refresher course when she drops a slice of pie into a customer's hoodie, but Ross saves the day by retrieving the pie for her. This apple pie spiced coffeehouse cupcake has its own wrapper keeping your fingers clean while devouring every last delicious bite. No hoodie needed!

DIFFICULTY: Medium
YIELD: 12 cupcakes
PREP & COOK TIME: 2 hours

CHAI SPICE MIX:
½ star anise pod
¾ teaspoons black peppercorns
½ teaspoon white peppercorns
1 tablespoon ground cinnamon
¾ teaspoons ground ginger
1 teaspoon ground cardamom
⅛ teaspoon freshly grated nutmeg
⅛ teaspoon ground cloves

CHAI CONCENTRATE:
¼ cup water
2 black tea bags (Tetley brand)

APPLE FILLING:
1½ to 2 tablespoons unsalted butter
2 small apples, peeled, cored, and cut into ¼-inch cubes. (Fuji, Honeycrisp, or Granny Smith)
1 teaspoon granulated sugar, plus more as needed

CUPCAKE BATTER:
1⅓ cups cake flour
1 teaspoon baking powder
¾ teaspoon baking soda
⅛ teaspoon salt
¼ cup plus 2 tablespoons buttermilk, at room temperature
1 black tea bag (Tetley brand)

½-inch piece fresh ginger, peeled and grated
1 teaspoon vanilla extract
2 large eggs, separated, at room temperature
½ cup plus 2 tablespoons granulated sugar, divided
6 tablespoons unsalted butter, at room temperature
2 tablespoons light brown sugar (break down any lumps)

TOPPING:
1¾ cups Whipped Cream (page 35)
2½ cups Sweet Buttercream Frosting (page 29), made with chai concentrate

TO MAKE THE CHAI SPICE MIX: Place the star anise and white and black peppercorns in a resealable plastic bag and smash with a meat tenderizer or rolling pin. Transfer to a spice grinder or mortar and pulverize. Add the cinnamon, ginger, cardamom, nutmeg, and cloves and strain into a clean covered container. The spice mix will last several months covered in an airtight container. Set aside.

TO MAKE THE CHAI CONCENTRATE: Heat the water to boiling and then turn off the heat. Add the tea bags and 1 tablespoon of spice mix. Steep, covered, for 10 minutes. Remove the tea bags and strain the liquid into a clean container. Set aside.

TO MAKE THE APPLE FILLING: Melt the butter in a medium skillet over medium heat. Add apples and cook until tender and light brown, about 4 minutes. Add 1 teaspoon of chai concentrate and the sugar. Cook until the liquid is absorbed. Add more butter if the mixture is dry and more sugar to taste. Remove from the heat and cool. The filling can be made 1 day ahead of assembly and stored covered in the refrigerator.

Continued on page 168

Continued from page 167

TO MAKE THE BATTER: Preheat the oven to 350°F.

Sift together the flour, baking powder, baking soda, and 1½ teaspoons of spice mix. Stir in the salt. Set Aside.

Warm the buttermilk for 10 to 15 seconds in the microwave so it's just warm enough to activate the tea, but not too hot or it will curdle. Add the tea bag and ginger and steep, covered, for 5 minutes. Squeeze the tea bag to remove all liquid, then discard. Cover and let steep for 10 minutes. Add the vanilla and bring to room temperature.

To make the meringue, in the bowl of a stand mixer fitted with a whisk attachment, or in a medium bowl if using a hand mixer, whip the egg whites to stiff peaks (see page 21 for tips on preparing meringue). When the egg whites are between soft and firm peaks, add 1 teaspoon of granulated sugar to help stabilize. The egg whites are ready when the whisk attachment is removed and the egg whites hold a stiff peak at the tip when turned upside down. If the egg whites are beaten past this point, they will look dull, grainy, and clumpy, and not be usable. Transfer meringue to a clean bowl. Set aside. Rinse and dry the stand mixer bowl and whisk.

Add the butter to the clean bowl and return to the stand mixer. Cream the butter using the whisk attachment, a few minutes. Add the remaining sugar and brown sugar and whisk on medium until the sugar lightens, about 3 minutes. Add the egg yolks, one at a time, whisking between each addition. Add a third of the flour mixture, alternating with the buttermilk mixture. Whisk in between additions until the ingredients are just combined without over mixing. Scrape the bowl frequently in between whisking. Spoon about a ¼ cup of the whipped egg whites into the batter and whisk until just combined. Remove the bowl from the stand and add the remaining whisked egg whites. Use the whisk to incorporate the meringue into the batter. Use a circular hand motion with a delicate touch. This step must be done by hand and not with an electric mixer or the meringue will deflate.

Place cupcake liners in a cupcake pan. Add an equal amount of batter to each liner in the prepared cupcake pan. Use a 1½-ounce, spring release portion scoop for even, flat top cupcakes, or 3 tablespoons of batter per cup. Bake 15 minutes on the center rack. Rotate the pan at 8 minutes. Cupcakes are ready when they spring back to the touch, or a tester comes out clean. Cool in the pan 10 minutes then unmold the cupcakes and transfer to a wire rack. Cool completely before filling or decorating.

To make the frosting, slowly add chai concentrate 1 teaspoon at a time while whisking into the sweet buttercream frosting. If the mixture looks like it's starting to curdle or break, raise the speed and keep mixing until it becomes creamy and fluffy. Chill and bring to room temperature before whipping or use immediately.

Remove a small center portion of the cupcake for the filling. Fill separate piping bags with apple filling, buttercream, and whipped cream and fit piping bags with a decorative star or round tip.

Fill each cupcake with a small amount of apple filling. Use the tip of your finger or a small spoon to push the apples deeper into the cupcake. Fill the rest of the cavity with whipped cream and make a small 1-inch center circle on the top of the cupcake to cover the hole. Finish frosting the cupcake with buttercream. Start piping on the outer edge of the whipped cream. Encircle the whipped cream center and pipe out to the edge of the cupcake. Place the finished cupcakes in the refrigerator. Serve the same day of making for the best taste. If making in advance, refrigerate and let sit at room temperature for 30 minutes before serving. This will allow the buttercream to soften and have a creamier texture.

MONICA'S PERFECT POACHED SPICED CANDIED APPLE

Everyone knows that Monica likes things to be perfect. Whether she is waking up in the middle of the night to move an out-of-place pair of sneakers or anxious about the beads of condensation rolling off a glass onto the wood coffee table, she takes everything to the next level. While you may not have the temperament of Monica, you can still make this elegant poached candied apple without stressing out or losing any sleep. It's the perfect dessert for impressing family and friends. Just leave all the obsessing to Monica. The recipe can be increased if you want to share. Or make one showstopping apple and eat your perfect dessert just the way you like without any distraction.

DIFFICULTY: Medium
YIELD: 1 candy apple
PREP & COOK TIME: 1 hour

FOR THE POACHED APPLE:
4 cups apple cider.
1 cup white grape juice
1 star anise pod
3 white or black peppercorns
Pinch of cardamom, or 2 pods smashed
½ cinnamon stick, about 2 inches, or ¼ teaspoon ground cinnamon
1 large apple, peeled and cored (Granny Smith or Honeycrisp)

FOR THE BASE AND GARNISH:
1 package store-bought pastry dough, thawed
3 tablespoons Salted Caramel Sauce (page 26)
One 3-inch round sugar or oatmeal cookie
¼ cup smashed vanilla cream– or maple cream–filled cookies (optional)
1 to 2 teaspoons unsalted butter, at room temperature (optional)
1 to 2 tablespoons finely chopped candied nuts

FOR ASSEMBLY:
Finely chopped candied nuts, for filling apple (optional)
Salted Caramel Sauce (page 26), for filling apple and drizzling (optional)
3 to 4 tablespoons Whipped Cream (page 35) (optional)
3 to 4 tablespoons ice cream, softened (optional)
1 Pirouline cookie or cinnamon stick
¼ cup candy crunch popcorn

TO MAKE THE POACHED APPLE: In a medium saucepan over medium-high heat, bring the apple cider, grape juice, star anise, peppercorns, cardamom, and cinnamon to a simmer. Add the apple, top-side down, so the poaching liquid will fully cover the apple when submerged. Poach the apple for 10 minutes, then turn it over and poach until tender, about 10 minutes longer. Remove the apple with a slotted spoon and let cool on a plate lined with paper towels. Reserve the liquid for a spiced hot or cold drink, or to poach more apples.

TO MAKE THE BASE AND GARNISH: Preheat the oven to 350°F. Use a leaf-shaped cookie cutter to cut out 6 leaf shapes from the pastry dough. Bake the leaf shapes on a sheet tray lined with parchment paper until light golden brown, about 10 minutes. Or make leaf cookies from the Rachel's Iced Baby Bunny Cookies dough (page 153).

Working freehand or using a ring mold as a guide, spread 2 tablespoons of slightly warm caramel sauce in the center of a plate, creating a 3-inch circle of sauce. Transfer the plate, uncovered, to the refrigerator to chill while you prepare the cookie base.

To make a cookie base, place a single large cookie on top of the caramel sauce on the plate. Alternatively, make a crushed cookie base with cream filled cookies. Add the cream filled cookies to the barrel of a food processor with 1 tablespoon of butter. Blend the cookies and the butter until thoroughly combined and they stick together when pressed between your fingers. Add an additional tablespoon of butter if needed and pulse to combine. Place a layer of crushed cookies on the caramel.

Continued on page 171

Continued from page 169

Spread the remaining 1 tablespoon of caramel sauce on top of the cookie base. Top the cookie base with 1 to 2 tablespoons of chopped candied nuts, creating a stable base for the apple.

TO ASSEMBLE: Cut the bottom fourth of the apple off to create a flat surface to place on the cookie and nut base. Dice the bottom into small cubes. Place the cut side of the apple on the center of the base. Fill the apple with nuts, caramel sauce, and/or the diced apple, as desired. Place the whipped cream or ice cream in a piping bag fitted with a large round tip to pipe ice cream or whipped cream into the center of the apple.

Add the Pirouline cookie to the center of the apple and position it as a stem. Add a pastry leaf near the stem and scatter any extra leaves artfully on the plate. Add the popcorn to the plate and drizzle the apple with the remaining caramel sauce. Enjoy!

NOTE: To save on ingredients, reuse the liquid to poach additional apples, poaching them in batches. The apples can be poached 3 hours before plating and stored refrigerated in a covered container with 2 cups of apple juice to cover and prevent oxidation. Several apples can be prepared and plated in advance. Add the whipped cream and ice cream, if using, on the side just before serving. Add the cookie stems, pastry leaves, and caramel popcorn just before serving as well so they stay crisp. Clear space in the refrigerator to chill the plated apples.

"COME ON.
WHEN WE WERE KIDS YOURS WAS THE ONLY RAGGEDY ANN DOLL THAT WASN'T RAGGEDY."
Ross

INDEX

TITAN
BOOKS

144 Southwark Street
London SE1 0UP
www.titanbooks.com

 Find us on Facebook: www.facebook.com/titanbooks

Follow us on Twitter: @TitanBooks

Published by arrangement with Insight Editions, PO Box 3088, San Rafael,
CA, 94912, USA.

A CIP Catalogue record for this title is available from the British Library.

ISBN: 978-1-78909-8-501

Publisher: Raoul Goff
VP of Licensing and Partnerships: Vanessa Lopez
VP of Creative: Chrissy Kwasnik
VP of Manufacturing: Alix Nicholaeff
Editorial Director: Vicki Jaeger
Designer: Leah Lauer
Editor: Anna Wostenberg
Senior Production Editor: Jennifer Bentham
Production Manager: Sam Taylor
Senior Production Manager, Subsidiary Rights: Lina s Palma

Food Stylist: Jaime Kimm
Photographer: Emily Schindler
Prop Stylist: Paige Hicks
Joey's Meanie Boat Sandwich Photographer: Kara Mickelson

Photo Art Direction: Amy King

ROOTS of PEACE   REPLANTED PAPER

Manufactured in China by Insight Editions

10 9 8 7 6 5 4 3 2 1

SERVICE